BEYOND THEOLOGICAL TOURISM

BEYOND THEOLOGICAL TOURISM

Mentoring as a Grassroots Approach
to Theological Education

Edited by
Susan B. Thistlethwaite
George F. Cairns

ORBIS BOOKS

Maryknoll, New York 10545

The Catholic Foreign Mission Society of America (Maryknoll) recruits and trains people for overseas missionary service. Through Orbis Books, Maryknoll aims to foster the international dialogue that is essential to mission. The books published, however, reflect the opinions of their authors and are not meant to represent the official position of the society.

Library of Congress Cataloging-in-Publication Data

Beyond theological tourism : mentoring as a grassroots approach to
    theological education / edited by Susan B. Thistlethwaite, George F. Cairns.
        p. cm.
    ISBN 0-88344-965-X (pbk.)
    1. Theology—Study and teaching—Illinois—Chicago.   2. Chicago
Theological Seminary.   3. Mentors in church work—Illinois—Chicago.
4. Christianity and culture.   5. Man (Theology)   I. Thistlethwaite,
Susan Brooks, 1948– .   II. Cairns, George F.
BV4070.C489B48   1994
207'.1'1—dc20   94-31784
                                                                          CIP

Contents

PART III
THEOLOGICAL AND PEDAGOGICAL REFLECTIONS

Foreword

Walter Wink

In 1982, my wife and I spent a sabbatical in Chile, concluding with a journey north through South and Central America. In 1986, we had a sabbatical in South Africa. In both cases, we spent a great deal of time visiting the slums, *barrios,* and *favellas* where the poor lived.

One day during our trip in South Africa, June turned to me and remarked dryly, "I suggest that for our next sabbatical we visit the United States."

Her point was well taken. We had spent in excess of twenty-one years on the edge of Harlem, and, yet, had almost no connection with the life of people there. We had attempted to address the problem of *de jure* apartheid in South Africa, but had done virtually nothing recently to counter the continuing *de facto* apartheid in our own land. We knew more about the marginalized people in Santiago, Rio de Janeiro, and Cape Town than we did about those living on the fringe in South Bronx or Watts.

Something of the same reflection went on with a group of seminary students, faculty, and administrators at these four Hyde Park seminaries. Only they did something about it. Having sojourned in Asia on a globalization project intended to widen the perspectives of the theological community, they concluded that their overseas experiences were not enough. What was needed was radical immersion in the troubled neighborhoods surrounding the seminary.

They learned quickly. They discarded liberal paternalism and a "we've come to help you" arrogance right away, and openly asked the poor, the homeless, prostitutes, and Native Americans to be their mentors—to teach them what to see, to give them a language, and eyes, and the capacity to listen.

Their report provides not just a summary of their experience, but reflections on what they learned, and a blueprint for others who are interested in transformative education. Such immersion experiences are truly baptisms in the best sense. People engaged in such an intense struggle for survival as the mentors in this project can help deliver our seminaries from their arid academism, scholasticism, and lack of context. A theology that won't play on the streets really is suspect, however hallowed. We are only at the threshold of what these teachers—"the least of these"—have to teach us.

Part I

INTRODUCTION

1

Beyond Theological Tourism

Susan B. Thistlethwaite

TOURISTS OF THE REVOLUTION

How do you provide pedagogy for oppressors? This question has bedeviled socially conscious North American theological education for the two decades since the energy and insight of theological reflection has passed so decisively to the two-thirds world. In the 1970s when everybody read Gustavo Gutierrez, we talked about "solidarity." Solidarity was supposed to mean a praxis of mutuality between those who have inherited national, race, class or gender privilege and those denied these privileges. While some, such as participants in efforts like Witness for Peace, did in fact learn to act out a mutuality which involved serious personal commitment and risk, for a much larger number of North American seminarians, clergy, and church members, solidarity rolled easily and trippingly off the tongue and came to mean relief efforts for Central America or South Africa. Central Americans on the receiving end of this charitable work joked about "tourists of the revolution."

The Plowshares Immersion Project made a decisive break with these ideologies of tourism. Robert Evans, when he came to conduct the orientations in Hyde Park for the foreign immersions, made this point emphatically. Bob emphasized that these were journeys unlike those anyone in the group had probably ever undertaken before, neither pleasure trips to "see the world" nor even traveling study tours, the academic's notion of a pleasure trip. They weren't business trips; they weren't missions. These were study/action trips, where the teachers would be our local hosts and where promises for changed behavior back home would be given and would be expected to be honored. The foreign immersions were a challenge to the notion of

3

tourism. The mentoring project, which arose as a response to the Plowshares initiative to construct a "local immersion," has continued and extended this trajectory of the rejection of tourism.

Tourism is only beginning to be examined seriously by political scientists and sociologists. Tourism, like the family, has been deemed a "private" activity and has never been subject to systematic scrutiny, and certainly has never been regarded as a topic for theological construction. Yet for a theological enterprise that is claiming the title "global" to ignore the ideology of tourism is a serious error. (See Chapter 7, page 107 below.) As Cynthia Enloe writes,

> Tourism has its own political history, reaching back to the Roman Empire. It overlaps with other forms of travel that appear to be less dedicated to pleasure. Government missions, military tours of duty, business trips, scientific explorations, forced migrations—women and men have experienced them differently, in ways that have helped construct today's global tourism industry and the international political system it sustains.[1]

Who travels for "pleasure" and why, how this dovetails with patterns in international economics, and its secularized cultural mission results[2] are all questions for investigation for a theology that would pretend to be global. The United Nations World Tourism Organization forecasts that by the year 2000, tourism will have become the single most important global economic activity.[3]

The impact of travel on the formation of consciousness could be found more centrally in literature when to travel meant to be an adventurer, when journeys were arduous, and to attempt to travel long distances meant that personal risk was involved. In the nineteenth century, popular literature became littered with "Mr. So-and-So's Egyptian Diary" or "Two Years in Darkest Africa" by Colonel Whomever. But the advent of air travel changed dramatically the amount of personal risk involved in foreign travel and in the latter half of the twentieth century the "twenty-one-countries-in-two-weeks" phenomenon has replaced adventure with endurance.

Why consider tourist travel as a means into a theological treatment of globalization? It was a truism (but none the less true for being a truism) of the early years of the modern women's movement that the personal is the political. This meant that what everybody assumes are natural relationships, such as the family, are really relationships fraught with power dynamics backed up by the more familiarly political realm of the public. This insight generated the examination of power dynamics in the family and led to the battered women's movement, the anti-rape struggles and eventually to the public disclosure of the extent of childhood sexual abuse. The theologies of the family that supported the view that the unequal power relationships between men and women were natural were subjected to scrutiny for their ideological blindness and their investment in the maintenance of inequality and exploitation.

In light of the tourist phenomenon, we need to engage in a similar kind of ideology critique: the personal is the international.[4] The fact of millions of economically privileged people engaging in international travel is not private and personal, a mere private pursuit of pleasure, as the dictionary defines tourism. There is a profound relation of this travel to patterns of international trade, debt, investment, treaties, and, ultimately, the new forms of colonialism. Furthermore, the appearance of objectivity, of non-involvement of the tourist, must be subject to critique.

What is the appeal of foreign travel to the economically privileged? In the place of adventure, of risk, of the connotations of journey for the passage of the human being through life, is the mode of observation of the exotic. This desire to see everything is similar to the prison Michel Foucault calls the Penopticon, where the inmates are arranged behind stories of glass walls; they are under constant observation. The purpose of foreign travel is to see things not seen at home and to contrast one's own existence with the exotic other. Being allowed no privacy is the torture the inhabitants of Foucault's prison undergo; it is a form of torture often employed in prisons around the world. The tourist who travels to see how others live without engaging them in any encounter but receiving service is just a little violation, it seems. But it is connected to the way power is distributed around the world. In fact, the exponential increase of international tourism greatly facilitates the other invasions of neo-colonialism as it prepares the inhabitants of an observed culture for their role as passive object and persuades the tourist of the superiority of his or her way of life "back home." In his brilliant travelogue on Asia, Pico Iyer writes

In 1985, another influence was also carrying American dollars and dreams to every corner of the world with more force and more urgency than ever before: people. Tourists were the great foot soldiers of the new invasion; tourists, in a sense, were the terrorists of cultural expansionism, what Sartre once called "the cool invaders." Scarcely forty years ago, most of the world's secret places were known only to adventurers, soldiers, missionaries and a few enterprising traders; in recent years, however, the secrets were open, and so too was the world—anyone with a credit card could become a lay colonialist. Nepal, which had never seen a tourist until 1955, now welcomed 200,000 foreign visitors each year; China, which had rigidly closed its doors for decades, had 11,000 tourists a day clambering along the Great Wall by 1985. The road to Mandalay and even the road to Xanadu were crowded now with Westerners—men in search of women, dreamers in search of enlightenment, traders in search of riches. In 1985, many Asians considered the single great import from the West, after Rambo, to be AIDS.[5]

But the quest to observe the exotic other has also, as Iyer so aptly describes his travels in Asia, become an experience in looking in a cultural mirror and, like fun-house mirrors, seeing one's own reflection, but with the contours grossly changed. And so, on our foreign immersions for the Plowshares Immersion Project, we went to a Dunkin Donuts in Taipei or a "Chicago Bar" in Hong Kong. In the mountains of the Philippines, where Dow Edgerton describes the brutality of so-called low-intensity warfare on the inhabitants, we turned a corner on our long hike and met a man on a donkey with a boom box belting out Madonna singing "Like a Prayer."

THE SELF/OTHER PROBLEM

How do I come to know the otherness of other people in a way that neither collapses their subjectivity into mine nor makes them into an exotic other? Philosophers and theologians have been puzzled for centuries over the meaning of the self/other relationship. For our purposes, the real question is not an abstract one of subject/object, but, "How can I come to know another and the world in which they dwell in a way that not only transforms us as individuals but enables us *together* to transform the world?" (*See* Chapter 6, Barbour, Billman, et al.)

Knowing another human being is qualitatively different from knowing a math problem or knowing that Monet was an impressionist painter. To know a human being is best understood as the mystery of encounter; this was first articulated systematically by Martin Buber in his description of the I/thou relationship.[6] On the same line with Buber, but even more specifically emphasizing the mystery of human mutual presence, is Emmanuel Levinas's theme of "face" (*visage*). This is the irreducible reality of another which I must recognize, whether it inspires love or violence. Face seems to mean not the fact of the other, but the fact that as a social being I must acknowledge connection to another when I look at his or her face and see that this is a human being like me and yet this is not me. This connection exists whether it leads to lifelong commitment or murder.[7]

There is a curious confirmation of the truth of what Levinas is arguing in regard to the face in the case of disease. Diseases that disfigure the face, such as leprosy, bubonic plague, cholera, or AIDS, have the capacity to inspire the imagination to horror and revulsion. At the same time, virulent diseases that do not disfigure the face, such as tuberculosis or influenza, give rise to little revulsion; in the case of tuberculosis, in fact, to a kind of romantic connotation of intellectual sensitivity. Influenza, which does not disfigure the face, is the worst "plague" the world has ever seen—surpassing in the numbers killed either in the great bubonic plagues of the high Middle Ages or the current AIDS crisis.[8] The face does assert a mystery of what it means to be human, and certainly of what threatens our humanity.

But the abstract way in which philosophers such as Levinas or Walter Farley, who employs the same metaphor of face to assert the possibility of human community in the "face" of threats to community through alienation and despair, is not yet helpful in overcoming the problems of theological tourism. Farley argues for the imperative to subjectivity the face implies. What transforms a simple encounter into an I/thou relationship (Buber) is that it is a *face-to-face* encounter.

The problem is that there are no faces per se. Where philosophers often fail in describing the human is in a too-quick jump to the universal. What is meant to be taken as common to human beings in a concrete way (we all have faces) is allowed to slide over into the liabilities of the universal. There is no universal face. There are only specific kinds of faces that have specific colors like dark brown, umber, pale yellow, ebony, coffee; and there are specific noses: large, narrow, wide, stub; and there are lips: full, thin, broad. The method of the general in regard to the human condition will inevitably mirror the old universals—white skin, narrow nose, thin lips—unless specific and historically rooted corrections are made over and over and over.

What makes the argument from the face for the mystery of the human encounter powerful is precisely the different topographies of human faces. What is threatening about the face of another is both the similarities and the differences. Differences mean that it might be possible to be human in another way than the way I have assumed it is "right" and good to be human. The other must be remade into a mirror of the self in order to reduce the danger that there exists more than one proper way to be human.

Travel brochures, to return to the tourist motif, often choose models from other countries who have more European features. In Asia, women and children are recruited for prostitution from northern Thailand or Burma because "they look the most white." There are now villages in the northern part of Thailand where this recruiting has been done so heavily that these villages have no children over the age of five.

But too great a similarity in another can also be threatening. If someone looks like me but has found a different way of being human, that way of being human is clearly possible for me too. This is at the root of much of homophobia, the fear of homosexuals. Heterosexuals often fear homosexuals not because "their lifestyle is so different," but because a homosexual in a power suit is indistinguishable from a heterosexual in a power suit. The barriers between self and other are threatened with collapse.

It is only the image of the "hardened self," as Catherine Keller puts it, that is threatened by the human ability to be a "permeable self."[9] Keller argues that the particularly Western symbolization of the self/other dichotomy has created an untenable transformation which requires that for a self to become *itself*, the other—often mythically portrayed as a female monster (e.g. Tiamat)—must be externalized and defeated. Keller lays part of the blame for this demonization of the other at the door of Christian theology.

> But let us not forget the theological sources of this transcendence. For it is the Christian tradition, in its conjunctions with Aristotelian philosophy, that bridges the long gap between ancient cosmogonies and theological existentialism, and that claims world-creating transcendence for human subjectivity.[10]

Promising directions in Christian theology, such as the incarnation, are not followed up for their refusal to divide the self and the world. Instead, there is an increasing emphasis on separation and control which becomes the common soil of the doctrine of the human being in the West.

TOWARD A DOCTRINE OF THE HUMAN BEING

It is a large claim for the project of mentoring to pose it as an alternative theological anthropology. Yet large claims are what is needed to shift the weight of theological education from the academic centers where it has been resting for several centuries. The theological import of this volume is that it proposes a different way of being human. This way of being human is predicated on the mystery of the encounter of self and other. But unlike many such claims for an I/thou relationship or of coming "face to face" with the reality of another human being, what is asserted here is that the human encounter is always in a concrete social context and that the encounter has a *purpose*, namely social and personal transformation.

The order of these is important, since we are countering a trend in liberal theological education which reduces everything to a "personal growth experience." As Yosh Ishida only half-jokingly remarked to potential participants in the first foreign immersion experience of PIP, "No growth." By this he meant that the purpose of the travel to Southeast Asia was not to be reduced to an intrapsychic experience, but was for the purpose of informing ourselves and others of the concrete conditions under which people struggle in these countries in order that we might, once back in the United States, press for our country's policies to aim more in the direction of human rights, economic equality, and democratic politics.

These problems of self and other have ordinarily, in philosophical and theological discourse, been abstracted from the concrete social conditions in which human beings, face and body together, are found. In all societies on the planet today, large differences exist in the material conditions in which different classes live—and there are significant differences within these classes of gender, race, and ethnicity (i.e. worldwide, women with dependent children are thirty percent more likely to starve to death than males in the same social class; an older African-American woman who makes $25,000 per year is not in the same social class in the United States as a young white male who makes the same salary).

The significance of gender, gender identity, race/ethnicity, class, national origin, or physical ability, to name a few parameters of concrete human life, has rarely been studied. It has only been with the advent of liberation theologies that the concrete differences in social location have even been taken into account in defining what it means to be human.

But virtually no one has done a theological anthropology that takes account of the *differences* in concrete social locations for the *transaction* of becoming human in the process of trying to transform the world. That is, how do we describe what it means to become human together when the real, material differences between human beings are made central? Furthermore, how is this relationship in difference constructed when we are engaged together in the act of world transformation? Do concrete differences and acting together constitute the possibility of a new human being? And what happens when we fall back, as we inevitably will, into ways of being the old human being?

MENTORING AS ANTHROPOLOGY

In the Christian West, the doctrine of the human being was, until modernity, subsumed under other headings, perhaps the doctrine of creation, or more often, fall and sin and the project of redemption. In the modern period, we have witnessed the decisive turn toward the human subject as a theological heading. From the nineteenth century on, to be a human being is to be a center of consciousness: one who knows objects by means of reason, who can know the laws of morality and who can exercise moral responsibility. To be a human being in the modern period has meant to be autonomous, to be in history, to be, quintessentially, a *self*.

To be an autonomous agent in history was taken to be a liberation from the constraints of an older authoritarianism that saw the human being as hopelessly mired in corruption and duty-bound, by virtue of this corrupt nature, to obey the laws of church and king, put on the earth to rule unruly human nature.

Freedom! What a concept. To be free to use your own reason, to create a better world, to question the authorities that pretend to rule you, and to be able to construct a more humane life. These were the promises that the nineteenth-century doctrine of the human being held out to the twentieth.

But instead, what happened? The same autonomy that was to provide us with freedom also caused us to abandon one of the very things that *had* been able to make us human in the long millennia of history: community. The individual was sought over against the community, and the whole marvelous concept of freedom degenerated into a quagmire of consumerism. To be free in the twentieth century is now the narrow realm of having lots of material goods and not needing to rely on anybody else. And for most of the world, this "freedom" bought in the Euro-Atlantic states and by the elites around the world has been at the price of the deprivation of the majority of the people in the world of even the basic necessities of life: food, shelter, clean water. Freedom and autonomy have had a terrible price tag: the material impoverishment of millions around the world and the spiritual impoverishment of the economic elites.

And so we must find another way to become human together. We must find a way to journey past the boundaries that have been thrown up between the haves and the have-nots and recognize that if anything like decent civilization is to survive, the means of becoming a community of selves must be found.

We have begun to learn some things. A doctrine of the human being must contain something of the following elements:

1. Body and Soul

Traditional theological formulations have seen the body as the opposite of soul. From Native American traditions, from feminism and womanism, have come the insights that to be a human being is to be both body and soul and that neither of these is "superior" to the other. From Latin Americans, South Africans, and African Americans, and from all who have been radically economically deprived, we have learned that embodiment is to be taken in the most concrete sense as physical well being, as the possibility of decent work, of civil and human rights.

Who symbolizes the body as fallen and alien from the soul more than the prostitute? Depaul Genska (Chapter 7) makes clear that what he, in a life devoted to ministry with prostitutes, and the students whom he helped to mentor, *learned from* those who work in the sex industry is "the deep mystery of personhood and its dignity." Despite lives of incredible victimization including physical, emotional, and sexual abuse, addiction, AIDS, and impoverishment, to name only a few, the prostitute manages often to be some kind of an ethical agent in her life. Perhaps she supports children or family members through her work. Problems of low self-esteem, poverty, and addiction do not yet completely eviscerate anyone's ability to work on the tasks of being a human being. Those who participated in the mentoring program with prostitutes learned that while sin and evil enter human life by means of violence and violation done to the body, transformation too comes through the human body, often in unexpected ways.

The person without a home, in the glib category we now call "homeless," is the essence of non-person in our material society because the homeless person has failed the one true test of being "free," *she or he doesn't own anything.* The participants who were mentored in the homeless shelters of Uptown in Chicago, according to Tony Gittins (Chapter 8), had to make the transition from "volunteer" to participant. They had to become "participant/observers," recognizing the integrity of the life they were entering and refusing the temptations to control the situation. As Gittins explains the method of participant/ observation used by the field of anthropology, we learn that body must be extended to mean the whole realm of embodied human life, the physical existence of human beings organized into cultures and subcultures. The use of participant/observation methods in the mentoring process has several rationales; a key rationale is to underline the validity of the social science approaches to understanding the concrete conditions of human life without which the contextual method cannot be understood.

2. Social Being

Human beings become human together. This is as true in the subculture of the homeless shelter as it is in the subcultures of church or seminary. This is a common theme in the chapters that follow. Gittins (Chapter 8) bridges this theme and the theme of embodiment. The ways in which people come together and form human communities differ profoundly from one to another. Entering into different social structures, as Claude Marie Barbour, Kathleen Billman, Peggy DesJarlait, and Eleanor Doidge (Chapter 6) say, in "respectful ways," is the first step in "cooperation without exploitation."

But it is only a first step. Awareness of the different social conditions in which human beings live is not yet the ability to engage in mutuality and to engage in social transformation. "Intellectual acknowledgment of difference does not always imply existential awareness of it." It is not possible to think your way into other people's social conditions, you have *go there* and you have to *be there.* But even this entering in and being with others, as in participant/observation, is a learning stage. "Commitment to work to change the ways our relationships are socially structured" is the product of entering into the neighborhood struggles, but also recognizing that one's social location of privilege has been a systemic contribution to the oppressions against which these marginalized people are struggling. In their poignant phrase, these authors note that these relationships "both wound us and set us free."

The social dimension of being human cannot be flattened to mutuality. To come to a complex understanding of what it means to be human together, we must come to understand and *to act against* the systemic structures which divide and set human beings over against each other and which destroy the possibility of community.

3. Purpose

Human beings are created with a purpose, and this purpose can be discerned through the events of our lives. As the chapters that follow unfold, they tell a particular story, as Dow Edgerton's (Chapter 2) narrative connection of the foreign and local immersions makes so vivid. From Manila at night to Genesis House for dinner, things happen to people who participate in these projects of globalization. When we tell what has happened we tell it in the form of a story which has a narrative structure and a dramatic purpose.

This raises the interesting point: is it narrative that gives structure to experience, or does lived experience have a narrative structure that a good story, a profound story, uncovers and offers back to those who live in history so that they can recognize and experience again the fact that life has meaning and purpose?

From the perspective of theological anthropology, we make the choice that life is a story of God and human beings and their relationship through time. This story has a structure of meaning and purpose and it is the function of telling the story to *get it right*. The dramas of human life that unfold in the telling and retelling of the story are the ways, sometimes in scripture, sometimes in more modern versions, that human beings tell—in order to know—who they are, what they have been, and *who they hope to become.*

As Dow Edgerton points out in introducing his story of the global and local immersions in which he participated, it is easy for focus to be lost in the myriad dots of experience that fill each day with people and institutions and tasks: ". . . how easy it is for people and institutions to become absorbed into the ten thousand thousand things and *forget.* So the stories which bear witness are not only told, they are *repeated* in order to remember. This is, it seems to me, at the heart of the liturgy of theological education: drama and story, eucharist and gospel, continually flowing back and forth."

In more traditional theological language, we might say that we are created so that God's will for human life can be known and the kingdom of God can be ushered in. We are not here without direction; history itself can reveal the purposes of God.

4. Temporality

Perhaps no shift in thinking about the doctrine of the human being is as characteristic of mentoring as the notion that human beings develop through time, and human transformation *takes* time. This point is first made by Clinton Stockwell (Chapter 4). The mentoring idea itself did not fall from the sky, nor were the structures which brought it into being in the particular way it happened in Chicago created in a moment. The Chicago mentoring model looks the way it does because of the history of urban ministry in Chicago and the structures for social change that were already in place.

As the mentoring progressed, the role of the theological reflection groups became increasingly important. Yoshiro Ishida (Chapter 9) points out the importance of keeping systemic issues in view—the "local/global connection"—as well as helping participants be realistic about what could be accomplished in the (still) relatively short time (nine months) of the mentoring program. The facilitators had to help the participants in the mentoring program experience their work as far larger and far longer than they had ever anticipated.

George Cairns, in describing the development of the mentoring model for local immersion (Chapter 5), notes how important it is to how trust develops between those outside the grassroots community and grassroots mentors as the outsiders "keep coming back." In his chapters analyzing how mentoring for transformation works, Cairns (Chapter 10) offers the fascinating insight that Jesus' mentoring should be likened to apprenticeship where the apprentice (disciple) only gradually learns the tacit skills known to the mentor. Truly transformational learning, where the learner is able to "see the world from multiple viewpoints and to shift among these perspectives with increasing skill," is a life project; it is not ever "accomplished" but, to cite Nelle Morton, "The Journey is Home."

BEYOND THE EXOTIC OTHER

Tourism depends on the appeal of the exotic other who is different enough to titillate, while not so different that one's sense of being a "hardened self" is threatened. The tourist can pop in and out of exotic locations with very little time expended and observe without participation. Far from being transformative, the tourist helps to keep the status quo by reenacting dominance.

Mentoring is a grassroots method for theological education which understands the human being in a different way than the "accidental tourist." The learner in a grassroots mentoring program enters slowly into a different culture and learns to respect its differences. The one who is mentored does not expect that he or she will immediately be given trust and responsibility. Larger systems of social and economic exploitation make a quick jump to trust impossible. Through learning to cross boundaries and cooperate with others without exploitation, the learner gradually is apprenticed in the ability to see from different points of view and to act in genuine solidarity with those who are marginalized in our society. In the mentoring relationship, both are changed, for a "face-to-face" recognition of basic humanity enables a process where becoming a new community is possible.

This process, because it is time-consuming and involves many people coming together to do difficult analysis and praxis, will *inevitably* be less than perfect. Perfection belongs to timelessness. People who live in time can only struggle with what is given to them at the times and in the circumstances in which they live. The kingdom looks like this: it looks like missing a commitment and having to apologize; it looks like resisting continuing power games and institutional stasis. It is only in the larger narratives, in the patient and revolutionary commitment to be human together despite all the warts, that we forge what Ada Maria Isasi Diaz has so aptly termed "the kin-dom of God."[11]

And so we begin with narrative—the story embedded in *some* stories—of how the foreign immersions flowed into the local immersion, and what it feels like to be in a mentoring relationship.

2

Stand by Me

Dow Edgerton

Stand . . . By Me!
Ohh . . .
Stand . . .
By Me!

CONTEXTUAL STATEMENT

I am a professor at Chicago Theological Seminary, where I teach courses in worship, preaching, and the practice of ministry. Birth: 9/7/48, Chicago Lying-In. Ancestry: English, Celtic fringe, Dutch, with some admixture of Native American. Married: 9/18/71. Children: two sons, born 1979 and 1982. I grew up in the Midwest, and with the exception of college I have lived in the Midwest all my life. CTS was the place of my own seminary education, so when I returned to teach in 1983 after seven years of parish ministry, it was rather like coming home. My academic background is chiefly in theological hermeneutics and literary criticism. My writing has been very textually centered; I write about the interpretation of texts: liturgical, biblical, literary, theological, mythological. I am particularly interested in the stories people tell to make a world. I am married. I tell stories to my two children.

My participation in the Globalization Project began with the first immersion trip—the Philippines, Hong Kong, and Taiwan—and culminated in the Chicago local immersion, three years later. My grassroots involvement for the local experience was with Genesis

House, a ministry dealing primarily with women in prostitution. My role in this book is that of a storyteller.

1

It can happen that, if you have come from sufficiently far, your mind and body get well pulled from their accustomed orbit. If you arrive in Manila in the dark hours after a midsummer midnight, your experience may be like ours. The clock says midnight, but your body says noon. Your mind begins to impose the usual order upon the material at hand, but it meets a subtle and powerful resistance which warns you off.

The dislocation and dizziness brought about by traveling halfway around the world in little more than a day have a way of placing brackets around the stories, categories, and worlds that we carry like so much heavy but invisible luggage. They have a way of bringing you to your senses to try to discover where you are. And then it can happen that you meet what you encounter on such a night with a kind, simple receptivity which otherwise costs a great deal of attention and concentration.

As you cross the city in those hours, the scale and scope of things is concentrated into a sequence of images picked out by the headlights, scenes performed beneath streetlight stage lights, glimpses through doorways and windows. Smells, sounds, the feel of what touches your skin.

The smell of jet engine exhaust, the ubiquitous airport smell, gives way to the smell of cars and trucks, less harsh because it is night and the roads are not too busy. Soon comes the unmistakable and unforgettable smell of woodsmoke mingled with an inexpressibly rich mixture of earth, moisture, decay, flowers, sewage. A floodlit billboard spells out in white script on a red background the name of a soft drink that has conquered the world. Beneath a streetlight, a young woman stands with one leg propped up on a bench. She leans forward to get a light from the man sitting on the bench, and, as we pass, she looks up and pulls back the hem of her short dress to show her leg. Outside a bar, three young boys—maybe eight or ten years old—sit on the curb and share a cigarette. Through the door comes indistinct dance music, and under a blue light—which seems oddly enough both stark and dim—a young woman dances alone in a cage. Three-wheeled bicycles, Mercedes limousines, tanker-trucks, spangled jitneys, a military convoy, a check-point. . . .

These are among the ordinary encounters as one crosses Manila at night. Each image, by its gravity and solitude, gathers itself into the weight of a symbol; each scene, by its stark glare and shadows, draws around it a larger drama; each glimpse, by its incompleteness and veiling, hints at a vast city hidden behind the door. Who is adequate to interpret such things? All you can do is pick a day, and start to tell the story of it.

II

It was a walk back into the mountains of Negros Oriental to visit a Franciscan clinic, but we've always referred to it as "The Long March." The province was one of the places where the Aquino government had apparently decided to demonstrate that there could be a military solution to the guerilla warfare that had been so significant a feature of life in the Philippines. Because the government had decided to demonstrate one kind of solution, the guerrillas had decided to make a demonstration of their own: if there was to be a solution, it was not the one the government had in mind.

This meant, therefore, that the area had become deeply militarized. Army, police, local militia, the New People's Army (NPA), village self-defense forces, religious and political paramilitary groups, private security forces, bandits, opportunists—all these and more were drawn into an intricate tangle of violence. In some ways it was worse than simple chaos. The knock at the door at midnight, the assassination at noon, the disappearance, the arrest, the accusation painted on the wall, the scooped-out grave—none of these were random and impersonal. Any and all of them were tied to reasons within reasons. Because you are Catholic, because you are Protestant, because you voted, because you didn't, because you have a job, because you don't, because you are in a labor union, because you are not, because you go to Bible study, because your child goes to university, because your neighbor is jealous of you, because your neighbor fears you, because you didn't lower your eyes, because you didn't raise your hand, because your son said "Yes," because your daughter said "No": reasons within reasons within reasons made any aspect of your life a possible cause of death. This is such a debilitating terror because it attacks a person through any and every decision and relationship, and this is the situation which had befallen the people who lived in the campo of Negros Oriental.

Our destination was a clinic up in the mountains. Operated by the Franciscans, it served the people of the upcountry. The people lived in farming villages, or small clusters of homes, or isolated shacks in the forest. Access was by jeep track and footpath. To walk out to the village at the end of the paved road took at least half a day. Much of the area was remote and impossible to control.

Because of its location outside the supervision of the army and well within the theater of operations of the NPA, the clinic had fallen under suspicion of aiding the rebels. That was hardly surprising, of course, and probably quite true. If you are in the midst of a war and help people who are sick or injured simply because they are sick or injured, you are *always* helping someone's enemy.

The trip to the clinic was, perhaps, less for us to *see* and more for us and the clinic to *be seen*. That is, a large group of international visitors has a way of calling attention and offering the paradoxical protection of visibility. To put it plainly, the anonymous and invisible are easier to eliminate, leave fewer traces, require fewer explanations. Perhaps our visit would help a little. Perhaps not.

Here was the plan: The bus would take us to the village at the end of the road. Our local contact and guide was unsure how far it was to the clinic from there, as he had never been there before. Maybe a half-hour walk, he thought, maybe an hour. The Toyota pickup would ferry the supplies and carry members of the group for whom the walk would be ill-advised. After spending the night at the clinic, we would come back to the road, make our way to a farming village and school nearby. We would stay one night there then return to our jumping-off point.

We had also picked up Father Rolie, a young priest whose parish reached from the big town on the coast all the way up into the mountains. It was an opportunity both for him to share what he had learned about ministry in such a difficult situation and to make his pastoral rounds to the congregations and base communities in the upcountry. He would come with us, introduce us and interpret, and celebrate the Mass.

It is a well-known truth that often the destination is not the goal. The goal is the journey itself. Your feet teach your head; you walk yourself into a different way of thinking, and not the other way around. For us, at least, this was true. The clinic, as it turned out, was not a half-hour walk over the hill. It was some twelve to fourteen kilometers distant, up and down the hills, past fields and homes, past goats and water buffalo, while the afternoon monsoon wind and rain came and went, came and went. We walked with pregnant women who labored and swayed up the switchbacks, with children returning from school with their books, with farmers who pushed supplies in barrows or deeply-laden bicycles, with bent laborers carrying loads by headstrap, and with young women who balanced laundry on their heads. Sometimes we could understand and speak to one another; often there was nothing to do but smile a greeting and walk along in silence, seeing, listening, smelling, feeling.

In time, the group of visitors stretched out into small clumps of walkers with congenial paces and gaits. Squalls would come and the people in roadside houses would motion for us to come in out of the rain. We'd ask how much farther to the clinic, and our host would get a worried look for a moment, then smile, and with a curving motion of the hand say, "Not far! Only two meters!" Father Rolie, in shorts, sandals, and T-shirt, told stories, stopped for brief pastoral visits, translated questions and answers.

As we came abreast of a small concrete house by the road, Father Rolie waved us over to meet the elderly couple who lived there. In the ordinary beauty of the place and ordinary discomfort of the day it had been easy to forget that we were walking in the midst of something extraordinary. Father Rolie asked about the couple's family. The woman looked down at her hands, the man looked off into the distance. At last she began to speak. The priest listened without interrupting. We listened too, although we didn't understand what she was saying.

It was easy enough, however, to *feel* what she was saying. Her voice sounded as if she was going down a list, naming, remembering, recounting. Then she would pause to shake her head or wipe her eyes, and go on to the next entry. All the while her husband gazed at the horizon. When she finished, Father Rolie asked permission to translate what she had said. She nodded.

"She was telling me about children and grandchildren who have been killed or who have disappeared," he said. "Some by the army. Some by the NPA. Some, no one knows why or how."

We all stood silent. The old woman began to weep. Then she looked up at a young woman in our group, a student. She took the young woman's face in her hands and brought it close to her own. It was as if she were talking to her own grandchild, it seemed to me. She wiped away her own tears and anointed the young woman's face with the moisture. Their faces were so close they must have breathed each other's breath. The old woman stroked that young face again and again as she wept and repeated a phrase we couldn't understand. She touched the young woman's forehead as if to mark her or bless her. At last, she turned away and walked through the door of her house; her husband followed her silently. "What did she say?" we asked Father Rolie. "She said, 'It's so dangerous, so dangerous,'" he answered. "'God protect you.'"

On we walked. There was the human truth of the situation. There was the human face of the fractured body that was the Philippines. Who is the neighbor? Who is the enemy? Who is the friend? Who can be trusted? What can be believed? These men we meet coming around the side hill, these men who stop and look at us from a distance, who are they?

Hours later, as we neared the clinic, the Toyota pulled alongside two of us. The supplies had been run on ahead, and the driver was circling back to distribute water and pick up any sore-footed walker who needed a lift. There was room in the cab so we opened the door to get in and ride the final kilometer. Still wet from the last squall, we were greeted by the shivery blast of the little air conditioner and the blare of the cassette player pumping out an American song.

> Darlin', darlin',
> Stand . . . By Me!
> Ohh . . .
> Stand . . .
> By Me!
> Stand by me . . .
> Stand . . .
> By Me!

When we arrived at the clinic, a large welcome banner decorated the hillside ahead of us. A crowd of people gathered to greet us. They began immediately to prepare for the Mass. In the clearing at the center of the compound, a table was laid. Upon it were offered not only the Eucharistic gifts but gifts of banana, corn, rice, coconut, sweet potato, and more: a bright and extravagant feast of good gifts of the good God. Father Rolie had disappeared as the preparations were completed, only to emerge from a small storage shed transformed. From a young man in sandals and shorts he had become a beautifully vested priest ready to preside at the celebration. The scene itself was striking: the gloriously laden table on the hillside; the priest of God and of the people, his bright robes brilliant against the dark greens, reds, and browns of the earth and the forest behind. Gathered in a broad semicircle children, women, and men stood, sat, and crouched. Babies bounced up and down, children were handed from hand to hand. Girls and women held hands or reached around each other's shoulder. Boys leaned back into the arms of other boys, and men into the arms of other men. Through the trees you could see the movement of still more people descending the trail from the far side of the mountain, arriving in the late afternoon shadows.

In the middle of the Mass was a time for testimony and requests for prayer. Whoever wanted would step to the microphone of the battery-powered PA and speak. Most of the messages were brief: thanksgiving for a child who was born, grief for a grandmother who had died, gratitude for a Bible study group, testimony of prayer answered, requests for healing. But one woman in particular kept the microphone for a long time, and as she spoke she seemed to become more upset and urgent. One of the clinic staff explained what was happening. "She's upset because people have been spreading rumors about her and the Bible study group which meets in her home. Some people are saying she's NPA. She's afraid and doesn't understand why people would say such things. She is making a vow that she and her Bible study care only about the Word of God and they want trouble with no one. She is pleading for people not to endanger her with gossip. She is telling the spies who are here to listen and believe her because she is telling the truth."

There was the human face of the fractured body again. One of us was there for an awful purpose. The Eucharist is not only about good gifts, but also about life and death, warfare and betrayal. It is a dangerous place to be, around the Table, so dangerous. God protect you.

III

The village of Magsaysay stretches along either side of the road linking the mountains to the coast. A school was there which enhanced both the size and importance of the village. Instruction went up through high school, so during the week there were many children and young people from the surrounding area on hand.

Here, too, Mass was a principal order of business when we arrived.

With American visitors, however, and so many excited children on hand, they decided to incorporate a talent show into the service somehow. Where one began and the other ended was unclear; celebration, after all (real celebration, that is), is celebration. Some children sang national songs and religious songs. Others put on traditional costume and did traditional dances. Some teenagers played and sang Beatles songs, performed upon a homemade guitar, the tuning of which I was completely unable to decipher. It was like the Table up at the clinic, only this time the children and their songs were the gifts. We all applauded deliriously.

In time, we, too, were asked to sing. Not being a group which made decisions easily or without much earnest soul-searching and negotiation, the request was potentially embarrassing. A hymn? A popular song? An oldie? A Sunday school song? For a rough collection of academics, administrators, trustees, and students the challenge of an open invitation was formidable. After a certain amount of sheepish shrugging and head scratching among us someone called out, "How about 'Swing Low, Sweet Chariot?'"

An inspired suggestion! We formed ourselves into a choir. One of us volunteered to hazard a likely pitch. Another stepped forward to direct. Off we went. By the time the second verse came around our group had warmed to the task. The director spanked along the tempo, and some free-form harmony and counterpoint developed. All in all we sounded pretty good, and finished with a sense of achievement. Then our hosts applauded heartily, cheered, and asked for another song.

Another song! Divine inspiration had saved us once, but to hope for twice was surely too much. The group members blinked at each other hesitantly. "Well, what else could we sing? I don't know, let me think." Then someone called out, "Let's sing that one *again*." An inspired suggestion. So we did.

Two moments of the talent show/Mass stand out with particular clarity. When the teenagers' youth group's turn came, they wanted to show us how well they could do American dances. A cassette player supplied the rock and roll, and four girls who had clearly been practicing together took to the dirt stage. Each of them danced alone facing the crowd. I don't know what the others saw and felt. Suddenly I was afraid. I had seen just such a dance not long before, after midnight, young women dancing alone in cages in Manila. Was this their past? Was that their future? Would these girls also take the road down to the coast and find their way to Manila to look for work or love?

Was a tinselled cage and a blue stage light and a pimp and drugs and death waiting for them down the road? The music ended; everyone applauded. The girls covered their mouths, leaned their heads together, and giggled. The grownups all beamed; the children cheered. Maybe. But maybe not. It is so dangerous. God protect you.

The second moment was for me one of the most remarkable experiences of church I can name. Announced were a group of teenagers who would perform a series of scenes. Each scene was an episode in the experience of a man of the village who had formed many of the Bible study groups in the area. A sort of director would call out a scene and indicate by some sentence or phrase the occasion which was to be enacted. A small slender man, maybe fifty years old, sitting in front of the dirt stage, took a soda can and rattled it sharply on the rocks. The young people played the scene through to its climax; the soda can signalled to stop the action. Then it would begin again with the next scene.

The teenagers looked like a typical high school youth group. The girls giggled; the boys smirked. They made eyes back and forth at each other, fidgeted, gave each other little shoves, and generally comported themselves as teenagers do.

"Scene one! The Bible studies begin!"

The can rattled. The young actors began a pantomime of a man moving from house to house, being received gladly, leaving behind small circles of people reading and talking. The can rattled.

"Scene two! The police come to question!"

The can rattled. Some of the boys became hard-faced and went from group to group. They bent down low and stuck their fingers in their companions' faces. They'd pull back a fist then laugh as the people questioned cringed. They appeared to find what they came for, wrote it down, and smiled wickedly at each other. The can rattled.

"Scene three! The first arrest!"

The can rattled again, and so it went. Each scene in turn enacted the escalating violence as the police attempted to link the Bible study leader to the guerrillas. At last it culminated in a group of these lovely fresh-faced boys, their expressions drawn into masks of brutality, enacting the beating and torture of the unnamed Christian worker from the village.

The can rattled once more. "Final scene! He returns to the village." The study leader limped down the stage to where the small groups awaited him. They touched his wounds and wept over them and kissed them. Then they enfolded him as if in a single embrace. They laid hands upon him and prayed over him. Then from the midst of them he stood up, and drew himself tall. He stepped away and began going once again house to house.

The can rattled for the last time, ending with a sharp smash upon the rock. "The work," called out the director, "the work goes *on*!"

All around us the people leapt up applauding and cheering. The teenagers applauded and cheered for themselves and the audience. We applauded and shouted. Grownups clapped each other on the back; children jumped up and down. The small man with the can looked around smiling. Then Father Rolie leaned close and whispered, "See him? The one with the can? That's the man. It's his story they're telling."

I was stunned. A colleague spoke quietly, "I think that is the most powerful pastoral care I have ever witnessed." She was exactly right. This community had taken a story of violence and terror visited upon them, and they had enacted it in the midst of the Mass, face to face with the mystery of the cross and resurrection. "Christ has died. Christ has risen. Christ will come again." They had taken this drama and placed it in the midst of another drama of violence and terror— and victory!—in which the terror, however awful it is, is overcome and the community of faith, in spite of the power of death, lives. They enacted the story in such a way that the children, instead of cowering, laughed. They enacted it in such a way that the teenagers' brutal masks were only masks which could be laid aside, not the permanent features of their faces. They enacted it in such a way that the grown women and men could witness their own story stand beside the story of Jesus.

Later, after everyone had eaten, we sat up late and talked to Father Rolie about what we had been seeing and hearing. We asked him, "How did you learn to do ministry in a situation like this?" He replied, "Well, first of all, you must understand that I didn't go to the regular seminary. You know, the kind where you go away and study with other priests and teachers then come back to practice what you learned. I was trained differently. Instead of going away to the teachers, the teachers came to us. We learned by doing ministry together."

IV

The final year of the globalization project centered upon a local immersion. The Chicago design (described more fully in Chapters 3 and 5) called for each participant to undertake a nine-month involvement with a local grassroots partner. The hope was to link the learning of the international immersions to our own contexts through an engagement in ministry as it is seen by the communities which are directly involved and affected. Mentors and reflection groups would offer guidance, support, and critical reflection. As a participant in the first immersion, and, more importantly, as one who was profoundly troubled in the best possible way by what I had experienced there and what it might mean for theological education, I volunteered to sign on for the final year. My placement was with a ministry called "Genesis House."

It seems a long way from the villages of Negros Oriental to Genesis House on the north side of Chicago, but it depends upon how you measure. If you measure in miles it is nearly halfway around the world. But if other kinds of connection count, it is only around the corner.

Genesis House is a ministry with women (and some men) who are seeking to leave prostitution. It was founded by Edwina Gately whose story is told in her book *God of the Forest, God of the Street.* Prostitution is so complex a phenomenon that even to *name* the different dimensions of complexity, much less analyze them or respond, is a frightening task. Sexuality, religion, economics, politics and policies, military power, gender roles, mythology, history, culture and tradition, violence, human development, race, law, personal and social pathology—reasons within reasons within reasons that are only just beginning to be seen and understood. No matter how complex the reality may be, however, prostitution has a human face. No matter how complex the analysis may be, at Genesis House it is with this human face that ministry is concerned. The work, therefore, is both broad and immediate: recovery programs, health and nutrition, childcare, art therapy, AIDS education, hospitality, emergency shelter, advocacy, job training, education, social skills, counselling, food pantry, public awareness, outreach in the jails, on the streets, in the bars. The work is done by staff, volunteers, and, of course, the clients themselves.

My experience at Genesis House began with a meeting with "Sharon," the woman who coordinates volunteers. "Sharon" is a person of terrific energy, who seems constantly in motion. She greets you, gives you a hug, talks as if she has known you for years and knows all about you, asks "How you *doin'*?" and basically leaves you spinning like a top. Her laugh can be heard all over the house. She knows exactly what she is doing and why.

I confess to being uneasy when I arrived at Genesis House the first day. What, after all, can I offer? I am middle-aged, white, middle class, the former pastor of a small-town church, an academic now, who teaches preaching, worship, and ministry. Granted, I have a fair bit of ministry experience, including settlement house and mental hospital work; I also have rather a lot of experience working cooperatively with women in ministry and education. But the world of prostitution and ministry with prostitutes was terra incognita for me.

Not knowing what else to bring to introduce myself to "Sharon," I brought my résumé. It seemed to make a certain kind of sense at the time. She needs to know who I am and how (and if) I might fit in and contribute—or be least in the way. So I tucked a copy of my curriculum vita under my arm and rang the doorbell.

Genesis House is indeed a house, a three-story graystone facing the street. You enter the foyer to find the living room back to your left, the dining room straight ahead, with the pantry and kitchen beyond. The upper floors are offices, meeting and living space. The basement has room for art activities, emergency beds, food pantry storage, and the usual basement things of an old house.

I sat in the living room and waited. Two young women, teenagers I guessed, were watching *The Little Mermaid.* They laughed at Ariel's silent attempts to get the prince to kiss her so she could remain human and get her voice back. I had seen the movie before, as I'm sure they had. It had made me uncomfortable when I first saw it, and I wondered then what the girls in the audience were thinking, about this little mermaid and themselves. At Genesis House, the movie was even more troubling than before. We all sat, watching the screen. Over the mantel was a painting of two women in tight dresses standing beneath a streetlight, waiting.

"Sharon" sat me down at the dining room table. We made mutual introductions. I handed her my résumé and waited as she looked it over.

Now, I am proud of my résumé. Not because it is so stunning, but because it really does reflect the range of interests, gifts, abilities, and accomplishments which define much of who I am. But just as the living room of Genesis House made me experience *The Little Mermaid* in a different way, in the dining room with "Sharon" my résumé also began to make me uneasy. It wasn't that "Sharon" was communicating any disapproval—she was always gracious and appreciative. *I* started seeing the pages with different eyes. What does that lovely article I wrote about the poetry of Rilke and the vocation of the poet have to do with those two women in the painting? What does that nice piece on Eliot's *Four Quartets* and his depictions of the Word have to do with the AA meeting going on upstairs? Of what possible interest or value or help to the women watching the video was my book *The Passion of Interpretation*? Or the courses I teach in preaching? Or my administrative experience in a seminary? Or whatever else was there? There was nothing there I was ashamed of, much I was proud of, but here I was feeling suddenly *embarrassed* and rather useless.

Truth to tell, I also felt a bit defensive.

"Sharon" turned the pages slowly, searching (I imagined) for anything that might be of use. She came to the last entry on the last page: "Interests and Hobbies." At none of the previous entries had her expression shown any sign of change: no widening or narrowing of the eyes, no nodding or shaking of the head, no arching of the eyebrows, or pursing of the mouth. Nothing to indicate interest or possibilities. But when she came to the last entry and read the list, one item caught her attention. "Sharon" looked up at me.

"You like to cook?"

"Yes, I do."

"You any good?"

"Yes, I'm a *good* cook," I answered, as if whatever sense of embarrassment I had over the other items on the resume had to be compensated by the defense of my cooking: a cook with attitude.

"What kind of food do you cook?"

"All *kinds* of food, from all over."

"Like where?"

"Well, like Mexico, Italy, Thailand, India . . ." I mentally raced along the shelf of cookbooks in my kitchen. ". . . Vietnam, France, Africa, China . . ." (I started to say Morocco but didn't because I'd only been looking at that one in the store), ". . . Middle Eastern, Greek, Cajun. . . ."

"Doesn't your wife cook?"

"I learned in self-defense."

"Can you cook for twenty people?"

Twenty people! But what could I say? It was all I had to offer.

"Twenty? Oh, sure. Sure," I nodded casually, as if I did it all the time, as if I could do it with one spoon tied behind my back.

"Sharon" explained how they had a Hospitality Night every Thursday, and not only the residents but other clients and volunteers were invited to come for supper. They liked to have something special on those nights to give people a sense of welcome and, well, hospitality.

They also could use some help with the monthly subsidized food pickup at the South Water market, she said. How about if I cooked a couple of times a month and helped collect the food?

Of all the things on my résumé, that was the one that seemed like it might help. I was glad there was at least one.

V

For the first meal I cooked, I decided upon something Mexican. I'd rub some pork loins with chili paste, roast them, slice them thin and lay them upon a bed of lentils seasoned mostly with chorizo, onions, tomatoes, and cilantro. There would be a big salad of mixed vegetables in a lime dressing, warm tortillas, and fresh pineapple for dessert.

As I worked out in the kitchen people would wander in and out. I introduced myself and responded to questions about what was for dinner. One woman asked if I was a chef. "No," I said, "I'm a teacher." "Where do you teach?" I told her. "Oh, that's nice. See you later." That's mostly the way it went. Everyone was very polite and friendly. Most were content to make small talk about food and leave it at that. As I stood stirring my pots and steaming my veggies, no one asked me to interpret some obscure passage of the Bible or explain a particular point of Christian doctrine. No one asked me for counsel or seemed particularly interested in much except the food I was preparing. All of this made perfect sense to me, of course. Relationships take time and who the hell is this guy anyway? But I wondered just how I should think about my role and what I was doing.

"Sharon" dropped in to check out the menu.

"Do you know why I asked you to cook?" she asked.

"Not exactly."

"You got to understand. Do you know what kind of relationship these women have had with men? Do you know what it means to meet a man who doesn't want something *from* you? Who does something *for* you? And doesn't ask anything back? Do you know what it means to meet a man who will do something to *nurture* you? And in a way that is simple and real and easy to understand? You got to understand, honey, you're not just here to *cook*; you're here to *feed* somebody."

It made perfect sense. Look at me and I could be anybody. I could be the john, the pimp, the battering boyfriend, the cop, the judge, the dealer, the condemning preacher, the abusive father. Or I could be just another person who doesn't give a damn. My role was to do something simple, real, and easy to understand, even without any words at all. My role was to be a man (specifically a man) who would feed somebody and be trustworthy about it. More than making sense, I decided, "Sharon's" idea was brilliant.

So that's how my work at Genesis House proceeded: through racks of Indonesian grilled chicken, platters of spaghetti with Bolognese sauce, cool Indian raitas, gumbo and dirty rice, bananas stewed in coconut milk. And sometimes sitting at the table, people would talk about the places the food had come from, and friends who came from there, too. And sometimes someone would sit down to find that food from her own people was honored upon the table, and she'd tell about wonderful dishes and meals that she had known.

Once I was making a big mixed salad to accompany Thai fried rice with seafood. The salad was to have red and green cabbage, tomatoes, green beans, sweet red peppers, bean sprouts, carrots, radishes, cucumbers, and whatever else I had found on sale at the Jewel's market. The dressing would be sweet, salty, and sour— sugar, fish sauce, and lime juice—fragrant with mint and cilantro, pungent with garlic, shallot, and chilies, and enriched with crushed peanuts. The ingredients were encamped in various corners of the kitchen (work space being rather cramped). A young woman came in and watched for a while. I was trimming, peeling, and slicing at the table and she offered to help. We sat working together, in silence mostly. We exchanged names. She was there just for a few days, she said, until some program opened up. She was nineteen, she said; I had guessed fifteen, if that. She started asking questions about cooking, why things were done this way or that. We talked about peeling broccoli and how to steam the stems and florets so they both came out crisp; we talked about scoring the skins of cucumbers to make a pretty pattern on the edge of the slices.

When the vegetables were all ready, I asked her to put them on the platter while I attended to the rice and seafood on the stove. I was pretty occupied for several minutes, so I didn't notice what was taking place behind my back. I turned to find her bent over the table shaping the brightly colored vegetables into a beautiful design on the platter. She was arranging dark against light, bright against pale, overlapping rings like fish scales, and minutely adjusting the edge garnish as if it were the frame of a mosaic. I had planned on just *mixing* it. I told her I thought she had made a lovely presentation. She said it was fun, and went back to watch TV. When suppertime came, I asked her to bring in the salad so everyone could see it in her hands, and so *she* could see it in her hands, and place it on the table.

That's the way it went.

VI

On Monday of Holy Week "Sharon" called. Hospitality Night that week was Maundy Thursday. I wasn't scheduled to cook that night—someone else was—but she wondered if I could come and lead a service at the dinner table.

By this time I had been cooking at Genesis House for six months. I always looked forward to going, and people were unfailingly appreciative and kind. My role was not one of leadership but of service. My place was in the kitchen and the table, and I was happy for it.

Now, however, "Sharon" was asking me to do something that was part of my profession and expertise. She was asking me to prepare a liturgy, not a meal. I was delighted, and a Maundy Thursday service was one which would adapt beautifully to the table. I said I'd be honored to help, and asked what she had in mind. A Passover seder, she told me. They had done something like that before, and the women had really appreciated it.

A seder? Here I thought I would be doing a service I *knew* how to do, one in which I knew my own strength and knew what to do with it. But a *seder*? I'd have to find some different Passover Haggadahs, study them, adapt them to the time and setting, and to the fact that neither I nor anyone who was likely to be there was Jewish. What about the meal, I asked? The director would take care of the lamb bone, bitter herbs, matzoh, and the rest, she said.

What could I say? It struck me as ironic and fitting. Still an amateur, after all these years. Sure, I can do a seder service. Do it all the time. For twenty.

That week I scrambled around to find resources that would give me ideas. The important thing seemed to me to find a way for us all to tell the story and enact the heart of the ritual: the story of liberation, and the ritual of remembrance. We hear the story with our ears; we see, smell, touch, taste, and eat the story with our hands and mouths. It also seemed important that the traditional prayers be recited, and recited word for word. As I read them over at my desk, I knew that part of their power was their ability speak across time and distance, their ability to speak distinctively and specifically to disparate people and situations. Sitting at my desk, I did not know how these words would sound at our table at Genesis House. I only knew that they *would* sound, and I would hear them as I had not heard them before.

The night came. The table was set. The plates were arranged. We told the story together, the story of captivity and escape. We recited some of the great words, ". . . This is the bread of poverty. . . . Let all who are hungry enter and eat; let all who are needy come to our Passover feast. . . . This year we are slaves; next year may we be free. . . ." I do not think I imagined this. When the words were spoken we all knew who they were about. Whoever else they were about, they were about us sitting there; whoever else they were about, they were about the women who were not at the table with us because they still dwelt in the house of bondage, and everyone at the table could call out their names.

Sitting at the table the realization came to me. I really do belong at this table now. Six months previously, had I been asked to lead worship, it would have been a formality, a nod toward my ordination and authority in principle. That night happened not because of my ré-sumé, but because of our relationship. Leading grows from feeding.

CONCLUSION

Remembering comes from telling. We remember by telling and tell in order to remember. Sometimes it may seem as if it were the other way around—that we remember, then tell *because* we remember—but I believe it is really the telling which comes first. We begin to tell and the story restores to awareness the hidden memory. Perhaps this is an experience we share. I begin to tell and discover that the story itself is doing the telling. The story begins to tell and I discover that I saw and heard and touched and tasted more than I knew at the time. I begin to tell and discover that by telling I am once again *there* where the story is, and that in this land of memory I can still walk and touch, see and hear. We begin to tell and discover that it is a *story* we are telling. Perhaps it begins with only an image, a sensation, the thinnest splinter of experience. But the image by its gravity draws story around it, or to say it differently, the strong image provokes one's own *need* for story. To tell of it one must somehow set the image in a story. From there the strong currents of meaning begin to flow. There is a story and it is linked to other stories, and, through them, to some great story in which these live and move and have their being.

My own conviction is that in the work of learning and teaching, globalization is founded upon a telling. It is, in the first place, not an analysis, method, or program. Those are vital and come in their proper time. But analysis, method, and program are themselves ways of coming to terms with stories which must be told. The stories come first and last. They are the source and judge of what one says and does in the name of globalization.

Let us insist, to push to point a little farther, that the stories themselves also have a source and judge: the dramas to which they point. The enacted dramas to which the stories bear witness are what matter in the end. It is from them that task begins. It is to them that analysis seeks to respond. It is for the sake of them that new methods are taken up, and by them that programs are judged.

This becomes a point of insistence because experience has shown repeatedly how difficult it is to keep focus, how easy it is for people and institutions to become absorbed into the ten thousand thousand things and *forget*. So the stories which bear witness are not only told, they are *repeated* in order to remember. This is, it seems to me, at the heart of the liturgy of theological education: drama and story, eucharist and gospel, continually flowing back and forth.

In the balance of events what I did was a small thing. Whether and how it was important to anyone else I can't say. There *was* something I was asking for in return, of course. I couldn't have named it well at the beginning, and even now I can only name part of it. It has to do with my own sense of vocation as a pastor and teacher. It has to do with my desire to help people who would be of help. It has to do with recovery of passion and surprise. It has to do with recovery of the sense of the holiness of every table.

I am grateful for those, represented in this volume, whose gifts of method and analysis transform such experiences as mine into structures and paths of education. My role is the role of a witness summoned to testify in a dispute about the truth. The truth I can tell is a story, and the loyalty I can offer to those whose lives enact the drama is to remember by speaking of them.

PART II

FROM FOREIGN IMMERSION
TO LOCAL IMMERSION
TO MENTORING

3

Globalization in the Hyde Park Seminaries

A History in Process

Susan Thistlethwaite
Heidi Hadsell

CONTEXTUAL STATEMENTS

Susan Thistlethwaite:
I am professor of theology, an activist on issues of violence against women, a wife, a mother of three sons, and a child of first-generation Hungarian immigrants. During our globalization program, I participated first in the foreign immersion trip to Southeast Asia, and, in the second phase, as a volunteer for Genesis House in the Court Advocacy program. During the trip to Asia, I began to get the idea for a book on prostitution in Asia and the United States, a book I am currently completing with my cowriter, Rita Nakashima Brock. I coedited this volume with George Cairns.

While the method of the theologies of liberation as contextual, communal, and concrete has informed my work for many years, the opportunities for grassroots theological work remain few in the academic centers of North America. This mentoring project has changed that, and I know it has changed me.

HISTORY

The stories in this book came about because there is an effort to make *change*. Mentoring as a grassroots approach to theological education came about as the result of many years of reflection in theological education throughout the United States on globalization. The term "globalization" came into wide use in theological education only in the 1980s. Prior to that, the term "internationalization" was commonly used. In the 1980s, the Association of Theological Schools (ATS) in the United States and Canada set up a series of committees to examine and facilitate the effort to make theological education more international. Surveys were conducted among the ATS member schools in 1983 and in 1989 in order to gauge what the schools' involvements in globalization were. In 1988 the ATS made globalization a major theme of theological education for the 1990s. A task force was appointed to work on support for globalization in the ATS member schools. Support included both grants for specific projects and the generation of literature on the subject.

The stream of globalization begins to bend specifically toward Chicago in 1987 when the Plowshares Institute, a private organization for justice and peace founded by Robert and Alice Evans, received a five-year grant from the Pew Foundation to promote globalization in theological institutions.

Plowshares was concerned about the provincialism of North American theological education in a rapidly diversifying Christianity and an equally rapidly changing world. They reasoned that one effective way to address the often excessively closed circle of contemporary theological education was to break the circle open through the provision of new experiences, both in the two-thirds world and locally, with careful and intentional reflection on those experiences, considering their relevance both to academic fields and to theological education in general in the United States.

More specifically, it was Plowshares' hope that direct contact with the realities of diverse groups of Christians, initially overseas in the two-thirds world, and then locally, would provoke critical self-questioning in the North American seminaries and a new openness to the experience and thought of Christians and non-Christians in very different situations all over the globe.

The travelling seminars were thus designed as a form of experiential education. They focused on engaged conversations with laypeople, theologians, NOGs, observation, and other forms of direct experience where possible, such as staying with local families. Theological institutions across the United States and Canada were invited to apply to participate in this experimental program. Eventually, thirteen schools of various denominations and from various regions were chosen as participants.

The thirteen seminaries which were chosen agreed to contribute not only considerable time and energy of faculty, students, trustees, and administrators to this globalization project, but to provide some of their own funding as well. The centerpiece of the project was three three-week overseas immersions—in Africa, Asia, and Latin America—in three years, and one local immersion in the United States in the fourth year for teams in each of the participating schools. The participants in the immersion experiences were to be the "leaven in the loaf" in their seminaries upon their return. As a result of their immersion experiences, they would, it was reasoned, have the passion and the interest to help provoke institutional change toward globalization in their seminaries in ways appropriate to each institution: curriculum, class bibliographies, library acquisitions, relationships with overseas seminaries, faculty appointments and exchanges, and so forth.

The participating schools were grouped together to make three larger groups that traveled together, and in many cases planned and carried out their local immersions together. The four participating Hyde Park schools—Chicago Theological Seminary, McCormick Theological Seminary, the Lutheran School of Theology, and the Catholic Theological Union—applied to the project and were accepted as a group. They therefore traveled together and planned and carried out their local immersion together as well. The globalization project was viewed by these schools as not only a valuable impetus towards globalization, but a golden opportunity to work on cooperation among these schools in Hyde Park.

Located within walking distance of each other, the four schools had a checkered history of cooperation. An umbrella structure for "the cluster" has existed for more than two decades, but it ceased to be an active centralizing agency (with a paid director and staff) when funding dried up for such ecumenical efforts in the early 1980s. Various projects "the cluster" had undertaken, and some even prior to its existence, had given these four seminaries both cause to hope that cooperation was a possibility, and reason to be suspicious of each other's commitment to cooperation. With this history, the Pilot Immersion

Project (PIP) was not only an external stimulus for institutional change toward globalization but also a way to work toward greater ecumenical cooperation within Hyde Park.

Certainly, these four schools were experiencing similar changes in the challenges of theological education, challenges that the PIP seemed well equipped to begin to address. Some of these challenges were related to ever more diverse student populations. The growing number of racial/ethnic minority students from the United States, as well as a large number of students from outside the United States, forced the question of greater diversity in the curriculum of the schools. Related to the question of the curriculum was the question of pedagogical methodologies adequate to the effective teaching of diverse student bodies, and the issue of the preparation for and cultural sensitivity of faculty to their students and their students' contexts.

WHY GLOBALIZATION?

Globalization can technically be traced back historically to Christopher Columbus. The "globalization" of Christianity followed the colonial expansion of the Europeans from the fifteenth century onward. Since the colonial mentality did not distinguish the gospel message from its cultural carriers, the missionary efforts in the period of colonial conquest by the European nations imposed European cultural values and practices on conquered peoples, with the concomitant devaluation of indigenous values and practices.

In the twentieth century, some of this mission activity began to be questioned, but an alternative vision has been slow to emerge. Often, especially for liberal Protestant denominations, eschewing old-style colonialist missions has meant retreating from contact with peoples around the world, except in approved "ecumenical" settings.

Thus, a major source of motivation for theological interest in peoples and cultures outside the Euro-Atlantic area was the contemporary desire to relate to them in new ways, breaking the violent patterns of the past. This was especially the case as Christians in North America witnessed the incredible eruption of the theologies of Latin America, South Africa, Central Africa, and Asia, the results of Christians involved in the rapid change and political and economic struggles in these areas. These theologies, often called "liberation theologies," but also sometimes referred to as "contextual theologies" or "indigenous theologies," were clear evidence that the very shape of Christianity was rapidly changing.

The rapid changes within Christianity itself, and not just outside it, are clear when one considers demographic data. In 1900, eighty percent of all Christians were Caucasian and lived in the Northern Hemisphere. By the year 2020, according to demographer David Barrett, eighty percent of all Christians will live in the Southern Hemisphere and will not be Caucasian[1]. Indeed, already, the fastest-growing Christian continent is Africa and the fastest-growing Christian country is South Korea. The globalization of Christianity is a fact; now North American theology is trying to keep up.

The term "globalization" can be used to mean this significant change in the center of gravity of Christianity and, in the United States, the attempt of Euro-American Christian churches to come to terms with that shift. In a report to the CTS faculty, Susan Thistlethwaite wrote, "Simply translated, globalization is the uncentering of Euro-Atlantic culture and theology." There is not agreement on this meaning of the term, however. "Globalization," in the participating Hyde Park seminaries, can mean primarily world mission and evangelism, ecumenical cooperation, inter-religious dialogue, a commitment to liberation and justice, or even urban ministry. Despite the diversity of meanings, dialogue between those involved in one or more aspects of globalization has been fruitful and rich. The dialogue continues beyond the involvement in the Pilot Immersion Project through the new Center for Global Missions, which directly involves three of the seminaries that participated in the Pilot Immersion Project, as well as several other seminaries, whose participation was more tangential.

THE LOCAL IMMERSION

The traveling seminar model was the centerpiece of the Pilot Immersion Project design. This model, with its emphasis on relatively short, but very intensive, trips, planned primarily by local hosts, has many strengths. It is virtually impossible for many participants to leave their families and jobs to go abroad for long periods, and the intensity of this model often produces significant changes in individual attitudes and behavior, sometimes dramatic ones.

When the Chicago cluster set out to design its local immersion, however, it did so hoping to overcome several weaknesses of the traveling seminar model perceived by a number of participants. These participants were concerned that the seminar participants, having traveled so far from home, found it difficult to view themselves as accountable to their local hosts in distant places, especially after they returned home and resumed their daily lives. For instance, the participants often promised local hosts that they would "tell the story" of oppression and struggle when they returned home. Once home, however, in the absence of easily-identifiable ways to tell the story, and in the press of daily obligations, this promise often went unfilled.

A related but not identical concern (again attributable in part to distance) was that there were few opportunities for the nascent relationships with local hosts to be ongoing or reciprocal. It seemed to many immersion participants that local hosts had given so much to them, but time and distance and complicated logistics made it hard to give in return, once home. Many immersion participants wondered if the distance and the differences in history, culture, and language of overseas hosts and situations masked or deflected the participants' attention from the similarities of many of the engagements and struggles of Christians at home. Thus participants asked themselves questions such as "Do we really have to travel halfway around the world to see Christians engaged in struggles for economic or political justice?" or "Should we not become more familiar with and engaged in our own local struggles?" Happily, a greater concern for local issues and context and the profound theological issues they raise was provoked by the immersion experience in distant places. As immersion participants got to know Christians in distant places acting in and reflecting theologically on their own specific context and issues, a greater desire to know their own political, social, and economic context was awakened in them.

The local Chicago immersion was designed in part to respond to these concerns. It was intended to have ongoing structures of accountability, which is far easier to achieve, of course, in local rather than international settings. It was also intended to benefit local hosts directly, and to perpetuate in a variety of ways the relationships begun in the local immersion. Finally, it was designed to enable the participants to get to know the political, economic, and social contexts in which their seminaries as well as their local hosts are embedded.

The original Pilot Immersion Project proposal describes the local immersion:

This pilot immersion project seeks to broaden the involvement of the seminary community with the "third world" at home. . . .

With the assistance of an outside consultant, the steering committee and immersion team members will seek to connect the
global perspective on the responsibilities of theological education to local situations of poverty and discrimination in North
America. . . . As in the international immersion, participants will
focus on the response of the church in light of serious analyses
of social, cultural, and economic issues that affect the structures
of poverty and discrimination.

Building on this description, the analyses of the international immersions discussed above, and conversations with local urban ministry
organizations and the people they work with, the Chicago local immersion design began to come into focus. This design came to be
called the "mentoring model," whose dynamics this book explores.

4

Education for Ministry in an Urbanized World

The Chicago Connection

Clinton E. Stockwell

CONTEXTUAL STATEMENT

I am currently a Faculty Associate and Internship Supervisor for the Chicago Metropolitan Center, an internship program for eight Christian liberal arts colleges. I have worked previously with several urban training programs. In New Orleans, I worked for the Urban Training Institute of the Trinity Christian Community, and, since coming to Chicago, I have been associated with the Seminary Consortium for Urban Pastoral Education (SCUPE), the Institute for the Church in Urban-Industrial Society (ICUIS), the Wesleyan Urban Coalition, the Urban Academy in Chicago, and the Chicago Center for Public Ministry.

I drew upon my experience as an educator and my knowledge of this and other North American cities in the development of the Local Immersion Project in Chicago. Chicago has a history of functioning as a laboratory to develop programs of this sort. Chicago is a "world-class" city, a city with global connections, ethnic neighborhoods, and problems of racial segregation, deindustrialization, and third-world conditions in some of its poorer neighborhoods. In Chicago, one can encounter not only issues of race and poverty but also structural realities, cultural diversity, and models of social change that are at work for the common welfare.

My role in the process was to participate in the design and imple-

44

mentation of the GTE program in Chicago. I was also invited to bring with me whatever resources I might have on the city and to suggest placement site locations whereby participants could encounter global realities in microcosm. This city, among others, boasts a variety of organizations that serve as models of engagement and social change. These include churches, social service agencies, advocacy programs, community organizations, and community development corporations.

The neighborhoods still represent what some have called "urban villages": distinct communities of Chinese, Mexicans, Italians, Greeks, Asian Indians, Koreans, Native Americans, Puerto Ricans, Poles, and Southeast Asians. It is thus possible to encounter the variety of urban people and community-based organizations that are at work in the city. It was my task to suggest such settings for the planning team. There are schools in Chicago where over sixty different language groups are present, and representatives of most of the world's 190-plus nations are found somewhere in the city. Hence, Chicago was a logical choice for such a globalization project, as the global village exists fully in Chicago, a microcosm of macrocosmic realities.

Urban training itself has been through many stages and has had many forms since the onslaught of the industrial revolution. To understand the place of Chicago in the flow of this development, we need to glance back at this history for just a moment. The concept of training for ministry changed dramatically when human life in the cultures of the Euro-Atlantic began to be organized around industrial production in an urban environment. Yet, a ministry directed *to* the city was slow to learn *from* the city.

URBAN TRAINING MODELS: AN OVERVIEW

Theological training models themselves emerged for the most part in connection with or in reaction to classical educational pedagogies. It was not until the mid-to-late nineteenth century that specific concerns emerged for training ministers for an industrial-urban society. Yet, for the most part, theological education for the city was still largely constructed on a classical model. From Reformation times, the preparation for ministry assumed that one had to master only the pastoral arts of preaching, biblical exegesis, historical understanding and liturgical practice to be effective. The model assumed that the best pastors or the most effective ministers were also disciplined scholars and orators. In Puritan New England, for example, the pastors were also considered community leaders and teachers of tradition.

This model pretty much held sway until the nineteenth century, when schools such as Oberlin were training not only scholars, but also fiery orators who could manufacture revivals. Training for revivals and evangelism began to complement the classical arts of rhetoric and interpretation. With Charles G. Finney, new measures were introduced that would help foment revival fires. While theological schools were divided over the utility of evangelistic methodology, the "new school" approaches seemed to triumph, at least among the evangelical schools.

The "old school" method might sponsor lectures on common themes such as abolition or women's suffrage, but the "new school" was interested in preparing lay evangelists to penetrate both city and countryside. However, it was the "new school" that combined revivalism with social activism. Finney was an ardent abolitionist and temperance crusader, as were his followers, among them Theodore Dwight Weld.[1] Abolitionist, temperance, Sunday school, and other mission models influenced by the Second Great Awakening were also influential in Chicago.[2]

By the end of the nineteenth century, pioneers were at work in the city, both in the invention of new models of urban presence and in the preparation of ministers. New models of urban presence such as city missions, rescue missions, the "institutional church" movement, and settlement houses, dotted the urban landscape. In the 1890s, with the beginnings of the social gospel movement, many schools such as the Chicago Theological Seminary attempted to combine academic training with the preparation for ministry.

In 1892, Dr. Graham Taylor was hired as a professor of Social Economics at the seminary, as he combined the new insights from sociology with traditional studies in theology, biblical exegesis, and church history. This led Taylor to develop Chicago Commons as a settlement house and laboratory for the training of ministers, social workers, and community activists. Taylor pioneered by using sociological methodology and the experience of living in urban communities as the basis for training people for ministry in social contexts. Taylor's efforts led to the establishment of the Chicago School of Civics and Philanthropy, which in 1970 became the School of Social Service Administration of the University of Chicago.

The settlement house and the rescue mission became two important para church forms of urban ministry until just after World War II. The settlement houses focused on environmental issues and advocated for social change, whereas the rescue missions, such as the famous Pacific Garden Mission in Chicago (founded in 1877), sought to change individuals, not the social system. The question of "system or souls" remains in current debate among advocates of social policy and practitioners of urban ministry.

In the late 1940s, three students from the Union Theological Seminary, George William Webber, James Archie Hargreaves, and Donald L. Benedict, developed the East Harlem Protestant Parish in New York City. East Harlem combined the social-service methodology of the settlement house with newer tactics of advocacy, political involvement, and community organizing. East Harlem began to question the root causes of racism and poverty in urban society with an analysis of social systems and urban public policy. Many seminary students would intern at East Harlem, learning not only how to pastor in a multiracial community, but also how to combine pastoral leadership with community activism.

THE CHICAGO CONTRIBUTION IN CONTEXT

In the 1960s, a network of "action training" ministries was started nationwide. In Chicago, this trend was represented by the development of the Urban Training Center for Christian Mission. A number of factors contributed to the tremendous activity that began around urban ministerial education in Chicago. A key factor in Chicago was the civil rights movement which led many clergy leaders to address head-on issues of race and poverty in inner cities. The visit of Dr. Martin Luther King, Jr. helped establish the civil rights movement in Chicago with concerns regarding such issues as voter registration, open housing, and hunger. "Operation Breadbasket" was an effort by black church leaders to address this problem, a forerunner of the Rev. Jesse Louis Jackson's Operation PUSH.[3] Unfortunately, King's death in 1968 set off a huge riot that ravaged the west side of the city.

Alongside the civil rights movement was the student protest movement which questioned classical educational methods, as well as United States domestic and foreign policy, particularly involvement in the Vietnam War. The culmination of this protest occurred in Chicago in 1968 as Yippies organized a mass demonstration in Grant Park during the Democratic National Convention. Who can forget the chant, "The whole world's watching!" The Chicago Seven trial of student leaders Tom Hayden, Jerry Rubin, and others characterized the public's reaction to student protests.

Finally, local tactics of community organization (like the work of Saul Alinsky or The Woodlawn Organization [TWO] on Chicago's South Side) contributed to more radical methods of training leaders who would also become community activists.[4] The civil rights movement and local efforts at community organization contributed to the unique character of urban training in Chicago, exemplified most notably in the Urban Training Center (UTC) of the late 1960s and early 1970s. The UTC gave divinity students training in skills of organizing, working in factories and industrial settings, exposure to other racial and ethnic groups in the city, and experiences on the street via the famous "urban plunge," and in political campaigns epitomized the nature of the training methodology.[5]

By the late 1970s to early 1990s, at least five models of training for urban ministry evolved. First, evangelical groups sought to combine creative ways to evangelize city people, including the poor. Such groups as Urban Young Life, Youth for Christ, and the Wesleyan Urban Coalition (Chicago) trained high school and college students in urban evangelism. Programs such as the Urban Ministry Program for Seminarians (UMPS) worked at training theological students. These programs combined relationship-building with social services and evangelism.

Second, beginning in the late 1970s, the Seminary Consortium for Urban Pastoral Education (SCUPE) was begun by several evangelical seminaries, including Calvin, Bethel, Northern Baptist, North Park, Trinity Evangelical in the Midwest, and the Acadia Baptist Seminary in Canada. The SCUPE model focused on the need of urban pastoral education. Founded by two urban pastors and a church denominational leader, SCUPE was particularly interested in the revitalization of the urban church. A full-year integrated curriculum was developed, combined with a year-long internship, mostly in an urban congregation. Over its almost twenty-year history, SCUPE has sought to answer the question of how to develop pastors and denominational policies to empower religious congregations in urban society.

Although SCUPE was founded by evangelical seminaries, the program has appealed to mainline denominations, and several mainline seminaries eventually joined the consortium. SCUPE's biennial Urban Congress regularly attracts about one thousand pastors, denominational leaders, students, and community activists, representing a wide spectrum of thought and practice.

Similar programs, roughly similar to the SCUPE program, have been established in other cities. For example, the Westminster Theological Seminary in Philadelphia, the Alliance Theological Seminary in Nyack, New York, and the Wesley Theological Seminary in Washington, D.C., basically replicate the SCUPE focus on urban pastoral education within the framework of one particular seminary, albeit with different theological and practical commitments.

It appeared that evangelicals in the 1970s were ahead of mainliners in urban training programs. However, like the East Harlem Protestant Parish, mainliners have been involved in training for urban mission throughout the post–World War II era.

A third model of training in urban ministry was started by mainline schools. This model combined a focus on congregations and urban pastoral education with the community activism model of the 1960s. Many, in fact, believed they were recapturing the old Urban Training Center model in the development of what became the Urban Academy in Chicago.

In Chicago, in addition to the Urban Training Center, the Institute for the Church in Urban-Industrial Society (ICUIS) in the 1980s offered training for pastors and denominational leaders in several of the major denominations, including the United Methodist Church, the Presbyterian Church, USA, the Unitarian Universalist Association, the United Church of Christ, and the Episcopal Church.

ICUIS was originally known as Presbyterian Institute on Industrial Relations (PIIR), but changed its name in the 1970s when it became more ecumenical. PIIR founder Marshall Scott provided training and internships in blue-collar work settings for seminarians for almost three decades.

In the 1970s, ICUIS became more of a research and documentation center under the leadership of Dick Poethig, reverting to a training-center model in the 1980s under directors Dick Simpson and Clinton Stockwell. Annual trainings in urban church ministry, community organization, and community economic development continued throughout the 1980s, but were discontinued for funding reasons in 1991.

For political and perhaps theological reasons, mainliners developed their own urban training programs as alternatives to "evangelical" programs such as SCUPE. In the early 1980s, several theological schools in Chicago combined to develop the Urban Academy. Rev. Donna Schaper was hired to develop the program. The Urban Academy was originally conceived as a think-tank that combined academic faculty and community leaders to help reconceive theological education. Meetings were held and papers were shared eliciting more discussion than implementation. These meetings used available space in the schools and in the offices of ICUIS because of the latter's history in research, training, and urban program documentation. Rev. Schaper eventually developed a number of programs, including classes for seminarians, "grass routes" tours of city neighborhoods and community organizations, issue-strategy groups, and a summer internship program.

In 1984, Rev. Schaper moved the office out of Hyde Park to Uptown, a diverse urban neighborhood, so that the training of leaders and reflection on urban issues could be done more in an urban context. Schaper combined her interest in feminist theology, community organization, and social activism in what, for many, was a very exciting program. Although the individual courses were poorly attended, the summer program burgeoned as a nationally-known program of training of ministers and community activists in urban society. Schaper continued the "urban plunge" model and sought to get students into urban neighborhoods in a variety of urban community institutions. Schaper numbered among her "sponsors" a wide range of groups including churches, community-based organizations, denominations, and even theological schools. The question of who owned the Academy (who would fund and control the program) ultimately led to its demise. Unfortunately, the administrative structure of the Urban Academy lacked clarity, and led to the reconfiguration of the Urban Academy as the Center for Public Ministry.

At this point, Donna Schaper moved to New York State to accept a pastorate. I was then director of ICUIS and decided to accept the job of developing the new Center. I renamed the summer program "Public Ministry in the City," and sought to develop other courses and a combined Introduction to Public Ministry course that would satisfy the schools' introductory course requirement. An urban term was launched that combined a course with internship in the city with such themes as health care ministry, education reform, and the church in urban society. However, the introductory course did not allow time for an experiential component. The proposed urban term demanded more time away from required classes than most students could give.

Hence the summer program became the most successful venture of the Center for Public Ministry, but was discontinued in 1992.

The fourth model has emerged which was not initially developed in Chicago. This model relies on indigenous urban church leaders. Chicago does have some experience at preparing indigenous church leaders, including the Chicago Baptist Institute, a training institute largely for African-American pastors. Also, the Trinity Evangelical Divinity School works with black urban pastors in a particular way, and this has some appeal to a small number of minority clergy in the city. However, a strong model that emphasizes the development of indigenous clergy does not exist in Chicago.

Each of the three previous models was specifically developed for Euro-American institutions and their students, or at least for middle-class students of the dominant culture. Realizing that many of the church leaders who needed training were African American or Latino, several programs emerged that sought to train leaders who were more indigenous to the city. The pioneer program for the training of indigenous leaders was the New York Theological Seminary. Bill Webber, formerly of East Harlem Protestant Parish, was hired by the seminary to address the problem of a declining mainline theological school, and how to redirect its purpose so that it more intentionally trained the pastors who were already at work in the city, most of whom were black or Hispanic. The result was a radical restructuring of theological education at NYTS to better address the needs of pastors already at work in urban congregations. Classes were offered at night and on weekends. The subject matter sought to address the practical needs facing working urban pastors. "Process" and discussion became primary teaching tools, along with the vaunted power of the lecture.

The needs of minority pastors, many lacking formal educational experiences, forced the development of several other training programs on the East Coast and elsewhere. These included the Center for Urban Theological Studies (CUTS) in Philadelphia and the Center for Urban Ministerial Education (CUME) in Boston. The former program combined the resources of Geneva College and the Westminster Theological Seminary to address the needs of mostly African-American clergy in inner-city Philadelphia. CUME was begun by NYTS graduate Eldin Villafane and was sponsored by the Gordon-Conwell Theological Seminary.[6] These programs assisted minority leaders as they obtained first degrees (B.A. and M.Div.) and while they were serving in existing urban churches. Essentially, CUTS and

CUME combined the evangelism and urban pastoral education models with "church growth" ideology made popular by faculty members of the Fuller Theological Seminary in Pasadena, California.

While the four models of theological education I have discussed are still functioning in but a few North American cities, a fifth model may be emerging. That is to say, with respect to churches in the city, some of the best "training" is not coming from theological institutions at all, but through programs that combine the training of church leaders, clergy and laity, with the older model of community organization.

Chicago too has its share of such models, many of which are church-based. Such organizations as the Midwest Academy, the Gamaliel Foundation, and the National Training and Information Center in Chicago; the Industrial Areas Foundation (IAF) in New York, Texas, and elsewhere; the Direct Action and Resource Training Center (DART) in Florida; and the Pacific Institute for Community Organization (PICO) and the Organize Training Center in California, develop "church-based" community organizations that address multiple issues of political empowerment and community development in cities. Training in community organization linked with churches has emerged as a national movement. The success of other groups such as Communities Organized for Public Service (COPS) in San Antonio and the Milwaukee Inner-City Congregations Allied for Hope (MICAH) has perpetuated the phenomenon.

"Church-based" organizing training involves the training of many pastors and lay leaders within the context of their churches and neighborhoods, and is basically unrelated to the more traditional preparation of church leaders in the theological schools. The theological schools have continued to stress the traditional arts, whereas training for urban ministry and public policy seems for the most part to have shifted to training organizations not directly associated with religious denominations or their schools.

Organizer training models seem to be much more connected with the realities of urban and rural congregations and seem to be more in tune with the emerging global, urban, and racially pluralistic realities of the modern postindustrial city. Further, many of these models are connected with religious congregations and the training employed equips not only the clergy but the laity and enables congregations to capture their role and their mission in the context of urban life. The success of "Church-based" community organization suggests that perhaps the schools could combine their efforts at training pastors with more grassroots models.

In Chicago, there are successful models of church-based organization as well. These include the Interfaith Organizing Project (Near West Side), Interfaith Community Organization (Mexican-American community in Pilsen), the Organization of the Northeast (Uptown-Edgewater), the Greater Grand Crossing Organizing Community (South Side), People Allied Under the Lord (PAUL) (South Side), the Developing Communities Project (Far South Side), and the Garfield-Austin Interfaith Network (GAIN) on the west side of the city. Each of these community organizations boasts a church-based constituency.

Historically, the former Urban Center for Christian Mission worked very closely with another Alinskyite entity, the Northwest Community Organization. In recent years, these community organizations have trained numerous student interns, many of whom have come from some of the several theological schools. Chicago also boasts perhaps the largest network of community development organizations nationwide, many of which are connected with two large umbrella groups: the Community Workshop for Economic Development (CWED) and the Chicago Association of Neighborhood Development Organizations (CANDO).

MENTORING IN CHICAGO AS A GRASSROOTS METHOD

While the established models have served churches well, new models are necessary, especially ones that address issues arising in the two-thirds world. The emerging realities require an innovation and a rethinking of how we train emerging pastoral leadership—clergy and laity. Such training must be developed with indigenous people everywhere. This is the essence of the mentoring program, Globalization for Theological Education.

The mentoring program in Chicago would not have been possible without the existence of organizations, such as those mentioned above, and of the long history Chicago has had with urban-based theological education. Yet it is clear that the older models which relied on direction from the seminary or university need to be combined with models, such as mentoring, that recognize that the power for change comes from the grassroots communities. The mentoring model identifies grassroots leaders and community-based organizations that are pointing the way to a new way of learning in a world that is increasingly urbanized and interconnected.

The Chicago mentoring program has not been alone in recognizing this shift. Similar models include the Center for Global Education at Augsburg College (Minnesota), the Women's Theological Center (WTC) in Boston, Massachusetts, the Emmanuel College Urban Clinical Pastoral Education (CPE) program in Boston, and the Berea College Appalachian Ministries Education and Research Center (AMERC) in Berea, Kentucky. These are all experienced-based programs that consider the unique dynamics of people in struggle, a common global theme.

In the Chicago mentoring program, students work in similar programs that address issues of global concern. These include SYNAPSES, a connector group that works on issues in countries such as the Philippines, Haiti and the Middle East; Clergy and Laity Concerned and its Racism Rehab Institute; the Medical Center Ministry, which works on a number of health care issues; the Northside Ecumenical Night Ministry, which works on issues that face street people; and Genesis House, a unique program that works with women in prostitution. These organizations seek to address issues that are of international significance. The Chicago Mentoring program successfully connects with these organizations, and students are able to learn not just from the people in leadership, but from the people "served" by these agencies.

COMMON THEMES

What do these latter programs have in common? While they are diverse and have different emphases, I believe that the experiential education programs, such the Chicago Mentoring Model, or the Women's Theological Center in Boston, or the others mentioned above, have several components that are strikingly similar.

First, most programs that seek to prepare people for ministry in urban or multicultural contexts stress the importance of *experience* and the so-called *"action-reflection"*[7] methodology. The action component identifies the phenomenon of experience and the encounter with difference, while the reflection component probes the meaning or significance of such encounters. The Chicago Mentoring model emphasizes the importance of experience and the reflection of that experience in dialogue with mentors in the field.

Internships in churches or community-based organizations are critical, as such experience provides the data for reflection and interpretation, which in turn allows issues and crisis situations to surface that become the data for discussion and pastoral planning for intervention.[8] Before we move to the "world as it should be," we must understand "the world as it is."

Second, many of these programs are linked institutionally to churches and judicatories, contexts, and situations. In San Francisco, the "Network Center for the Study of Christian Ministry" was intentionally linked to congregations in the city which provide the *context* for learning ministry. Context is important, and one cannot learn the concepts or skills in ministry in a classroom removed from the urban environment. Contextualization means that the learner takes seriously the issues one actually encounters in a specific geography, neighborhood, or "turf." For intercultural trainers, this is similar to what is called "area analysis," the attempt to understand the facts, trends and issues that are specific to a particular place or context. Contextualization also affects the way that learning takes place. To maximize learning, courses, small groups, seminars, and workshops are hosted in local neighborhoods which encourage students to relate their faith to the urban environment and issues that are endemic to that milieu. Learning thus becomes more concrete—practical and relevant to real issues, and abstract, theoretical in nature. Such training is "reality-based," rooted in the stories and experiences of people in struggle.

Third, *teaching is interdisciplinary.* The world that we live in is complex, and systems and issues run into each other and are not neatly compartmentalized. A holistic and comprehensive vision of ministry and ministry-preparation needs to bring experts and practitioners together for dialogue and mutual interchange. In the 1960s, leaders in "action training" programs spoke of a "pedagogy of reversal." That is, "experts" in ministry issues are not just advocates, university scholars, or even seminary professors, but people who are most affected, including the homeless, welfare mothers, the unemployed, people with AIDS, and so forth.

In Chicago, we have done workshops with homeless people as leaders. We play a simulation game with the "Women for Employment Security" to show students the reality of living on public aid. The workshop is conducted by women who are welfare recipients. Finally, students have been exposed to the work of resident administrators in the Resident Management program of a local public housing project. Many people in public housing have excellent organizational and administrative skills. In the Chicago mentoring model, representatives of other religions, other races, and of the diversity of people that comprise the city are mentors to the participants, including people with AIDS or people in prostitution, the "lepers" of postmodern society.

Fourth, such programs generally have *small groups* to allow people to discuss issues, articulate their theologies, and to identify skills for ministry. In the programs I have been associated with—six in two cities—the small groups have been the critical point where integration of learning takes place and where theory and practice are brought together. The programs address issues of personal identity in a multicultural world, just as they explore strategies for ministry and the resolution to problems encountered on the placement site. It is in the small-group setting where students are helped to develop a systemic analysis in order to place their particular experiences within larger patterns of economics, race, gender, or of national and global politics.

Small groups are essential, because the best education for urban ministry or for cross-cultural situations in a global world should be process-oriented, not just content-oriented. Content is of course critical, but our world and our understanding of it are very dynamic and in constant flux. A process orientation to learning assumes that a sharing of stories, a reflection on one's experiences, an identification of one's feelings, and a reevaluation of one's beliefs are essential. Small groups provide the best forum for these reflections to occur. They also help in the building of relationships in community, and in the important supportive environment necessary for people to confront the many critical issues that face people who care.

Fifth, students must have opportunity to learn *public skills.* Often, the placement site provides opportunity to learn skills such as community organizing (much of which today is "church-based"), administration, fund-raising, leadership development, program development and implementation, advocacy, and networking or coalition building. These are not the usual skills taught in seminaries, but they are essential for effective ministry and leadership in the parish. Other skills must be encouraged, including public speaking, public relations, and how to influence public opinion, as well as how to relate to a culture different from one's own.

Public skills are essential in a world that values private life over public life. In a culture that vaunts individualism and privatism as the ideal, "people power" is often an unrecognized resource. Skills to bring people together, to identify and channel scarce resources, and to develop concrete strategies for social change are essential in a society that seeks to marginalize or divide those whom we might call the powerless or the disenfranchised—the numerous populations being created in global society.

Finally, the Chicago mentoring model, while it has elements that have been learned from all these programs, both historic and contemporary, which have employed experience-based education, adds the dimension of *relationship building*, personal contact over an extended period of time between mentor and student. This extended personal contact is what enables that which is finally transformative to occur. Even in church-based community organizations such as Pilsen Neighbors, relationship building is seen to be primary. "One-on-ones" are essential building blocks for any people's organization. Networks with allied organizations build power and credibility. The practice of active listening is empowering, as it affirms and validates the stories of others—and builds community among strangers in the process.

These six components—experience, contextualization, interdisciplinary teaching, reflection in small groups, the learning of public skills, and relationship-building—have their origins in the "salad bowl" (not "melting pot") of the variety of educational expressions found nationwide and in Chicago. Like cities and the variety of ethnic groups that comprise a city, educational theory and practice have a certain distinctiveness depending on their context.

Other cities and other regions will have had different histories, and their approach to mentoring as a grassroots method will have to be drawn from the histories and experiences of individual communities. So the dressing put on the salad will be different—perhaps with Southwest spices or Northeastern thickness—but we are beginning to understand the basic composition. The method must be contextual, it must endure over time, and it must connect people with one another and engage them together in personal and structural transformation.

CONCLUSIONS

Chicago has functioned historically as an important laboratory for urban and cross-cultural training programs. Its past models of city missions, settlement houses, and various urban training programs have made use of the city's geographical, socio-economic, political, and cultural significance. The city has been studied for decades by several leading university departments, and today stands as a microcosm of macrocosmic realities, owing to the current transformation of the city, as the economy in particular shifts from an industrial-manufacturing society to a service, high-technological society. These transformations have forced numerous economic dislocations, and globally have either fueled or attracted an overflowing stream of immigrants from the developing world, especially Asians and Hispanics in the post–World War II era.

Yet, the city also boasts numerous community-based organizations, activist congregations, community development corporations, advocacy agencies, and grass-roots groups who have responded to dislocation, stratification and demographic pluralism in creative ways. The mentors identified in the Chicago Pilot Immersion Project have largely come from these organizations. These mentors have a long track record in addressing a multitude of issues facing urban dwellers, including hosts of new immigrants. Various models have developed in this city, among others, including social services, community-building, human-rights, political-enfranchisement, and economic-development organizations. Mentors have not only shared their story but have also shared their vision and their expertise in the process.

We have learned much from this project. Most importantly, we have learned the importance of a good connection, an important social network, a guide or exemplary program that serves to point to a new way of understanding the diverse cultures that populate such large cities as Chicago. Community-based organizations and their leaders are most in touch with their communities, and can share the most regarding the situation, needs, vision, and strategies by which dreams become reality. Mentors not only contribute their stories but also challenge the way "outsiders" see their world. They also challenge our values, beliefs, assumptions, and predispositions.

In this process, we have come to acknowledge the importance of relationships. It is not enough to have a toolbox of ideas which one somehow transports to another situation, however noble or well-intentioned. Rather, it is in relationship with people who are already there that real solutions to concrete problems emerge. Active listening is not only an important way of learning but it is also dignifying, affirming, and even empowering. We have learned the importance of sharing stories, of hearing the voices of others, especially the voices of those most affected by injustice, marginality, or discrimination.

We have also learned the importance of social analysis, or critical thinking. It is easy to see the homeless, refugees, or addicted people as individuals—to blame those people for their plight. While we all have responsibility to address the situations in which we find ourselves, it is important to see the larger picture as well. Mentors have raised questions for us, asking us if perhaps certain policies, systems, and social structures do much to exacerbate particular problems. As sociologist C. Wright Mills put it, we need "sociological imagination," the ability to connect the plight of individuals with the larger social trends and structures that cause the troubles of individuals. People are as much sinned against as they are sinners.

We have learned the importance of context, of a social situation, or, as some theologians have called it, the *Sitz im Leben* (situation in life). It is impossible to understand another person's reality or the troubles she or he faces without paying attention to his or her situation, the concrete reality faced by others. Similarly, answers to troubles cannot be projected without first understanding the context, and without really appreciating the understanding and hopes of the persons most directly affected. We might call this the "felt-need" principle. Activists, missionaries, and organizers have learned many hard lessons, among them the critical importance of the needs articulated and experienced by the subjects.

Finally, we have learned from mentors the importance of imagination. Yes, we must first name the world "as it is," reality as experienced and understood by those most affected. However, it would be too easy to feel powerless and hopeless in the face of oppressive systems, the biblical principalities and powers. Imagination is important as people hope and dream for a new way to live and relate to one another. Biblically, we all know that people perish without a vision. Empowered people are those people who are not only encouraged to dream, and dream wildly, but they are those who have the resources and abilities to somehow realize those dreams. Mentors are ones who help us understand the world as it is. Yet, mentors are also our primary resource for seeing the world as it should be. As people, young and old, dream new dreams, then we are helped to move toward a new future. Perhaps we will then be able to sing a new song. We will then be able to set up residence in a new land as those no longer strangers.

5

The Theory and Practice of Transformative Education

The Chicago Mentoring Model

George F. Cairns

CONTEXTUAL STATEMENT

I served as the coordinator of the Local Immersion Project in Chicago from the initial development of its grant proposal until its completion in May of 1993. My contracted time commitment averaged about one-half day per week during the two-year period that encompassed the planning and implementation of the project. One of the major reasons for my selection was my roles as an adjunct faculty member at the Chicago Theological Seminary, as a minister of urban mission serving the Peoples Church of Chicago in one of the most diverse neighborhoods in North America, and as a member of an ecumenical community (Shalom Ministries) that is engaged in cross-cultural training and linking people across classes. Another reason was my experience as a clinical psychologist and mental health administrator who has had extensive experience working cross-culturally.

This chapter will detail the development of the project and the explicit overall strategies the planners and I implemented as the project developed. Of course, the process is examined here only through the eyes of one viewer. Other perspectives are represented by the other authors in this book. It is clear that the strategies we used in the project changed as the project developed. These strategies will be examined. What I will stress here are the systemic elements of transformative education. I will examine the dynamics of individual transformation in Chapter 10. The outcomes of the project will not be examined here. This is the contribution of Yoshiro Ishida (*See* Chapter 9).

INITIAL ASSUMPTIONS

From the very beginning, the seminary planners of the Local Immersion Project acknowledged that this project was designed to encourage change among the economically and socially privileged in one North American educational context (four seminaries in the Hyde Park neighborhood of Chicago) by immersing these people in the "Two-Thirds World Next Door" that begins within three or four blocks of their institutions. The explicit strategies were to encourage both individual and systemic change within this seminary community. The values of mutuality with local hosts, critical ecumenical examination of theological issues, ecumenical cooperation, and long-term planning, as embodied in the overall goals of the GTE project (*See* Chapter 1), were all part of this mix.

Early on, a strategy to view the entire local immersion process as an initiatory event emerged, one that has many elements of the rites of passage found in many cultures. This process, described by Victor Turner,[1] Arnold van Gennep,[2] Mircea Eliade,[3] and others, is applied here to describe a journey that is taken by a few participants to bring back new understandings to the larger community. We, as planners, were sensitive to the notion that marginalized people, by definition, live their lives in the stage of liminality and that the model of journey itself presupposes a stable community in which to be reintegrated. Many persons are persecuted for this very liminality.[4] In order for this process not to become just one more means of sustaining division, we took care to mitigate the privilege that we as planners and participants enjoy. We specifically addressed the privileges of class and education, which provide a relatively stable community for reflection and reintegration, by adopting an overall strategy of being led by the members of the community whenever possible. Similarly, we were concerned that, if globalization is not to become just one more ideology among many, with the journeyers becoming only one more elite who have one more intellectual credential with which to separate themselves from others, efforts must be made to erode these power relationships.

Thus we attempted to utilize a dialogical process and encouraged such processes at all levels during the project.[5] By this I mean that we attempted, whenever possible, to engage in a process of mutual education, a bottom-up planning process, where the powerless had the lead, where the grassroots mentors taught the participants, where the participants and the grassroots mentors taught the cross-cultural trainers, and where these three groups taught the Local Immersion Planning Committee (LIPC, the seminary/community group responsible for facilitating the local immersion). The resulting process was one where the overall goals of the project were in tension with a coevolving contextualized agenda that developed during the project.

THE GRANT DEVELOPMENT PROCESS

A critical and unexpected challenge occurred early in the grant development process. A planning committee of local cross-cultural trainers challenged the notion that an intense fourteen-to-twenty-one-day immersion could, in fact, provide mutuality in the Chicago context. What quickly developed was a profound change in the direction of the project, generated by these people who are bridge-builders between the seminaries and grassroots communities. These are people who live in both worlds. They act as community educators for seminaries. Their cooperation was necessary for the project to be implemented. They wished to recontextualize the project to better fit the Chicago situation. The details of this planning stage are described in Chapter 3 and I will not report them here, except to say that a radical shift in strategy occurred during this stage. A bottom-up planning process developed, which we used throughout the project.

This bottom-up process was structurally embodied in the development of a planning group, the Local Immersion Planning Committee (LIPC). The LIPC originally consisted of the bridge-builders between the seminaries and the grassroots communities who took part in the early planning process. Later, seminary representatives joined the group. Ultimately, the seminary administrators responsible for the overall conduct of the GTE project in Hyde Park, the Seminary Coordinators, permitted this group to make all tactical decisions regarding the Local Immersion Project. The LIPC had primary responsibility for planning the two stages of the project: recruiting participants and the immersion itself. The LIPC met monthly during the two-year period of planning, recruiting, and immersion. Please see Appendix A for a description of the overall administrative structure of the Local Immersion Project, located, as it was, in the larger GTE Project.

What follows is an overview of the implementation of the project and then a detailed description of each of the project stages. I will attempt to describe the project and the significant shifts in the project content as it unfolded from a dialogical process.

THE PROJECT AS IMPLEMENTED

Overview

By the time we implemented the project it had two stages: recruiting participants and mentors and matching mentors with participants, and the academic-year-long immersion itself. Once the four seminaries agreed to the overall design of the project, we formally began recruiting in December 1991, with a mailing to all seminary students, staff, faculty, and board members, describing potential community sites.

The immersion stage began the following September. Participants in the project covenanted to work with community mentors for an average of fourteen to twenty-one days during the period of the project, which began in October with the initial orientation and which ended with the March 14, 1993 celebration; to attend monthly ecumenical reflection groups; and to attend the initial orientation and the final celebration. During the Local Immersion year, a fourth phase emerged—a celebration that would encompass the entire Hyde Park GTE Project including as many participants from the overseas immersions, the local immersions, and other interested parties as possible.

The Recruiting and Matching Stage

1. Recruiting Community Mentors. The recruiting followed naturally from the networks in which the LIPC members already existed. Three cross-cultural, urban training organizations were represented on the LIPC: The Chicago Center for Public Ministry (CCPM), Shalom Ministries, Inc., and The Seminary Consortium for Urban Pastoral Education (SCUPE). Two additional members of the committee were individuals who had long-term commitments to theological reflection and "hands on" ministry with marginalized people: Depaul Genska, ministering with women in prostitution (*See* Chapter 7) and Anthony Gittins ministering with homeless women (*See* Chapter 8).

The philosophy of the LIPC regarding these individuals and organizations was "to do what you do best," with coordinating and communication being the major responsibilities of the LIPC. Much of this organizational style was influenced by Leonardo Boff's notions.[6] Boff describes an organizational structure for the church that employs a collaborative, needs-defined organizational structure rather than one based on power or authority. Ultimately, this way of being a community reflects a contemplative world view.[7] By this I mean that individuals, to use Boff's terminology, become organic participants who are "implanted" within the new communities, and eventually are "implanted" back into their home communities, rather than "transplanting" themselves during the immersion, later to be "transplanted" back into their home communities. This implies a more organic process of deeply interconnecting with the lives of the others across cultures and to then act as a means for these connections to be extended back into the seminary communities.

Since many of the members of the training organizations were also members of the LIPC, it was easy for us to develop a collegial style. Some of the LIPC members also performed several roles. At least three LIPC members acted as site mentors. Thus, while the organizational chart in Appendix A generally depicts the lines of communication, the process was more complex and organic than can be represented in such simple models.

2. *Community Training Organizations.* "The Chicago Center for Public Ministry is the ecumenical cooperative program of Chicago Theological Seminary, Community Renewal Society, Lutheran School of Theology at Chicago, McCormick Theological Seminary and Meadville/Lombard Theological School."[8] As its name suggests, it is an ecumenical program that has provided a variety of public ministry training experiences for the seminary community over many years. It was an outgrowth of a similar organization, the Urban Academy. I would characterize this program as one in which, typically, active site mentoring development is combined with regular group reflection on systems issues.

The second organization, SCUPE, has also acted as a training program in urban and public ministry. "The Seminary Consortium for Urban Pastoral Education provides specific programs of study in the area of urban pastoral education. SCUPE works cooperatively with Chicago area churches and community agencies and is committed to the development of competent and creative leaders who both understand and can work with the realities of power, poverty, and pluralism found in cities."[9]

SCUPE typically combines careful mentoring development with group reflection process.

The third organization, Shalom Ministries, has been training people in urban and cross-cultural ministry for approximately fifteen years. It is an ecumenical Base Christian Community that engages in cross-cultural ministry and mission training.[10] This organization holds careful mentor development and intense group reflection as its standards. (In Chapter 6 there will be more details on this process.)

3. *Individual Mentors.* As mentioned above, two members of the LIPC acted as site mentors, because of their long-term work in particular places. Depaul Genska provided mentoring for three participants at Genesis House, the house of hospitality for women working in prostitution (*See* Chapters 2 and 7), and Anthony Gittins mentored two participants working with homeless women at a women's shelter operated by Residents for Emergency Shelter (*See* Chapter 8).

4. *Recruiting Participants.* The initial plan was to recruit a significant number of seminary community people to act as participants in the local immersion process, since one stated overall goal of the GTE Project was to have "a core of over 300 faculty, administrators, students and trustees directly involved in the project who continue to influence seminaries, professional associations, and church bodies as they provide leadership for ministry in a global context."[11] In this spirit, we originally sought forty participants for the Hyde Park local immersion. Ultimately, twenty-eight participants began the project and twenty- five completed it.

Our initial intent was to recruit a minimum of twenty-four participants who were permanent or semipermanent seminary community members (administrators, faculty, and trustees), and sixteen students, equally distributed across the four participating seminaries. We quickly found that this plan was inadequate, based, as it was, in the assumption of relative homogeneity of the seminaries themselves. Instead, we found that the four seminaries brought different gifts to the process. Given each seminary's particular historical context, especially with regard to globalization issues, we found that there was significant involvement, with people involving themselves in ways which we had not originally anticipated. Perhaps this can be best illustrated

Table 1.
Number of Faculty, Administrators, Board Members, and Students Involved in the Local Immersion Project by Role (count duplicated by role—some persons had more than one role in the Local Immersion Project).

SEMINARY AFFILIATION

ROLE	CTS	CTU	LSTC	MTS	TOTALS
FACULTY					
1. Participant	2	0	4	2[1]	8
2. LIPC Member	1	2	2	3	8
3. Small Group *Facilitator*	0	1	0	0	1
TOTALS	3	3	6	5	17
ADMINISTRATORS					
1. Participant	1	0	0	1	2
2. LIPC Member	1	1	0	0	2
3. Small Group *Facilitator*	0	0	0	1	1
TOTALS	2	1	0	2	5
BOARD MEMBERS					
1. Participant	1	0	2	1	4
2. LIPC Member	0	0	0	0	0
3. Small Group *Facilitator*	0	0	0	0	0
TOTALS	1	0	2	1	4
STUDENTS					
1. Participant	4	4	4	2	14
2. LIPC Member	0	0	0	0[2]	0
3. Small Group *Facilitator*	1	0	1[3]	0	2
TOTALS	5	4	5	2	16
TOTALS					
1. Participant	8	4	10	6	28
2. LIPC Member	2	3	2	3	10
3. Small Group *Facilitator*	1	1	1	1	4
TOTALS	11	8	13	10	42

[1]Includes one faculty spouse

[2]While no students were permanent members of the LIPC students joined the committee at several times during the process to address specific issues.

[3]Alumnus of LSTC

by the roles seminary community members took in the project. Table 1 describes the composition of seminary involvement by nature of role in the Local Immersion Project.

It became clear early on that it would be difficult to recruit a total of forty participants as anticipated. We rethought the recruiting process and engaged people to join in the project as their skills and commitments led them. Since some faculty, staff, and students (or former students) had already been deeply involved in the cross-cultural reality of the city, we engaged them to participate with us based on their particular gifts. For some this meant acting as a mentor or a bridge-builder between the community and the seminaries. For others it meant planning and integrating the process into seminary curricula so some students ended up receiving field placement credit for the project. Others did many different things.

The point is that, as the project developed, we continued to fundamentally redesign the project as we shaped our agendas and incorporated those of others as they joined us. The sense of this evolution is captured in the following words of Don Jose Maria Arizmendiarrieta, founder of the Mondragon producer cooperatives in the Basque region of Spain: "We have learned that theory is necessary, yes, but it is not sufficient: We build the road as we travel."[12] In our case, the theory was provided by the overall goals of the GTE Project; the road we built together was the immersion experience where no one stood outside the process.

5. *Matching Participants with Sites.* Just as there was heterogeneity of participants in this process, so, too, the matching process took into consideration potential participants' ongoing ties with the communities involved, their particular interests, and the needs of the community organization. Appendix B provides a more detailed listing of participants with sites.

Our initial intent was to involve participants for an average of fourteen to twenty-one days during the immersion. As we contextualized this "level of effort" with both participants' and site mentors' needs, we found a wide range of different arrangements. For example, some participants contracted for more intensive involvement over one quarter; others were on site weekly, biweekly, or had varied schedules. We attempted to contextualize the notion of mutuality by balancing an equivalent time commitment project-wide with the particular needs of the community mentors and participants. So here too we evolved some of the basic assumptions of the project, that a commitment of one to one and one-half days per month would be the norm for the project, but that the form this took would be determined from the bottom up by the grassroots mentors and the participants.

The Immersion Stage

1. Initial Orientation Phase. We held the initial orientation Saturday, September 19 and Sunday, September 20, 1992 in the Uptown neighborhood of Chicago. It combined orientation to the GTE project itself, a discussion of general global issues, presentations which related these issues to the local context, and immersion in one of the most diverse communities in North America. One sign of the diversity of this community is that more than sixty languages are spoken in the neighborhood high school. These experiences were combined with the testimony of grassroots mentors and shared experiences of participants in the overseas immersions. Please see Appendix C for a schedule for this orientation. At the end of the orientation, participants met with the people who would supervise their site placements.

The general movement through the weekend was one of transition from the environs of Hyde Park to Uptown, and from our usual academic communities into the ecumenical reflection groups which would be the major interconnecting link for participants during the mentoring phase. Markers of this transition were initial talks by seminary professors, later talks by community people, and finally a commissioning ceremony and celebratory meal.

2. Mentoring Phase. The mentoring process involved at least two levels—first with on-site mentors and second with peers and a facilitator in ecumenical reflection groups. Given the bottom-up philosophy that underlay the project, each mentoring individual and organization was encouraged to "do what you do best." In some instances, this meant that the community training organization, via trained community mentors, provided access to the mentors, made infrequent checks with the participants, and were available otherwise for backup consultation only as needed. One organization, Shalom Ministries, utilized a more intensive and intentional group and individual mentoring process for all participants placed through that agency (*see* Chapter 6 for details).

2.a. On-Site, Grassroots Mentors. A total of twenty-eight people were placed in community sites. These sites were supervised by both individuals and community training organizations. Appendix B describes the range of sites, as well as individual and community training organizations acting as supervisors, and a list of the sites themselves.

Two individuals (*See* Chapters 7 and 8) and one organization (*see* Chapter 6) provide a detailed look at how this process developed in their contexts. In each situation, varying with the resources available, attempts were made to contextualize the process for everyone involved. We were not always successful.

2.b. Ecumenical Reflection Groups. Each month, the participants met with facilitators for ecumenical reflection. The meetings initially took place on Fridays from 3:00 to 6:00 P.M. I met with the facilitators and LIPC and Seminary Coordinators for processing for approximately an hour following the small group meetings. Initially four such reflection groups were formed. One group facilitator was nominated from each participating seminary. Selection criteria for the facilitators included skills at theological reflection, sensitivity to cross-cultural issues, and experience facilitating small groups. Ultimately, three groups continued from about mid-year as a result of smaller numbers of participants and one facilitator's relocation.

The format of these meetings varied. The general format was for the four groups to meet together for a brief devotion and general announcements, followed by meeting in assigned groups for reflection. Both individuals and reflection groups acted as leaders for devotions. The ecumenical small groups reflected on individual issues raised by participants on their sites, linking these issues to larger issues of globalization and redesigning the process as we went on.

In the latter part of the year, the format changed slightly with two plenary sessions following the devotions. These sessions were requested by the participants and facilitators to focus the entire group's attention more directly on cross-cultural experience, crossing boundaries, and long-term systems change. We found that systems issues were not being addressed in as focused a way in the reflection groups, and we also discovered that attendance was dropping, so we redesigned the last three sessions of these meetings in an attempt to revitalize the process.

In the first plenary session Dr. C. Adrian Heidenreich, an anthropologist and educator who has worked with North American Native peoples for many years, facilitated a discussion that centered on theoretical and practical issues crossing cultural boundaries. He described the difficulties which arose when a play about contemporary Native American life was presented in an Anglo institution. Differences in time, mutuality, and respect in the two cultures created many barriers and difficult encounters as this play was produced.

Dr. Claude Marie Barbour and Dr. Eleanor Doidge facilitated the second session, a month later, which examined individual and systemic transformation as engaged by the Shalom Ministries community. Out of these meetings grew the design for the ending celebration for the local immersion, and also the plan for a celebration to bring closure to the GTE Project as a whole.

Local Immersion Celebration Phase

The completion of the local immersion was marked by an afternoon session in which participants and facilitators tied up loose ends in the small ecumenical reflection groups where we participated in an ecumenical worship service and where we ate a celebratory meal together. The worship service was designed and conducted by volunteers from the project.

Grassroots mentors were invited to this celebration and several attended. They added much to the day. As one example, during the worship service, one local mentor who lives in a single-room occupancy hotel asked that Luke 4:16–21 be reread. She repeated each line as it was being read and said "Yes" at the end of each. It was one powerful moment of "a gift of the other" in unexpected ways.

While this celebration on May 14, 1993 acted as the final marker for the local immersion, the impulse to develop a celebration that would include as many people as possible took place during the last few months of the local immersion. This project-wide celebration was both an outcome of the project and a source of further insights about how the process continued to evolve and to connect in new ways with the larger seminary and local community.

GTE Project Celebration Stage

One week after the end of the local immersion, a celebration titled "Celebrating Our Journey, Visioning the Future" was held at Catholic Theological Union. Strictly speaking, the local immersion was completed the week before this event, but it directly led to this event, so this process and outcome will now be considered. Please see Appendix D for a schedule of the day's events.

About seventy people attended the celebration. For many people, this was the first time that they had seen the overall dimensions of the project. Presentations of the overseas and local immersions were combined with forward planning in small groups. During the small-group discussions, it was generally agreed that the globalization process should be continued. Several people expressed residual concerns that structural changes needed to be made if the process were to continue. Several people said this was the first time that they had engaged in a discussion of their seminaries' long-term plans for globalization with the mix of faculty, trustees, staff, and students present there that day. Some raised concerns whether a continued globalization process could be maintained without a broad-based, ongoing planning process.

The concluding worship service provided several surprises. Designed to be a service of repentance, celebration, commissioning, and covenanting, this service crossed boundaries of class, religion, culture, and race. In the spirit of the project, participation was encouraged of members of the gathered group. At one point, the entire congregation joined in a Taiwanese song and circle dance led by Rev. James Chang, a student at CTS. The joining at the table for a celebratory meal symbolized both the connectedness of the group in the process, and the ending of one process and the beginning of another.

This two-year process of planning and implementing a local immersion in Chicago has taught us many lessons. These lessons are explored in the chapters which follow. Let me say here that, for me, the most important lesson is that no one can stand outside the process if it is to be successful. As we were led by the spirit in this project each of us was challenged to view ourselves differently. Each of us was required to suspend our usual roles in order for the process to work. Each of us ultimately was called to act—and to be—differently with one another. To the extent that we individually and collectively allowed ourselves to open to this possibility, we see the world differently. You can evaluate how well we met this challenge as you read the accounts that follow.

6

Ministry on the Boundaries

Cooperation without Exploitation

Claude Marie Barbour, Kathleen Billman,
Peggy DesJarlait, and Eleanor Doidge

CONTEXTUAL STATEMENT

The four of us have chosen to write this chapter together as a way
of reflecting our commitment to the collaboration and mutuality
suggested by the chapter title. We were brought together from diverse ecclesial backgrounds and institutions through participation
in Shalom Ministries and the partnership between Shalom and the
Global Theological Education Local Immersion Project (hereafter referred to as LIP).[1]

Claude Marie is a professor of world mission at the Catholic
Theological Union and McCormick Theological Seminary. She is an
ordained Presbyterian Church (USA) minister, a former missionary
in South Africa, and founder of Shalom Ministries and Community.
She served on the LIP Planning Committee and as a Shalom mentor
and Theological Reflector.

Kathleen is an assistant professor of pastoral theology at the Lutheran School of Theology at Chicago. She is an ordained United
Methodist minister and formerly served two cross-cultural congregations in Trenton. She became a member of Shalom through participation in the LIP. Her LIP placement was at the Marjorie Kovler
Center for the Treatment of Survivors of Torture, where she assisted
staff working with Cambodian refugee women.

Peggy (White Cedar Woman) is from the Arikara tribe in Fort Berthold, North Dakota. She is a respected elder in the Native American community in Chicago and serves as a member of the boards of directors of many Native American organizations. A member of Shalom Ministries, she has been a mentor to many theological students and lay people interested in cross-cultural ministry and service in the Native American community.

Eleanor is an associate professor of cross-cultural ministry in a joint appointment with Catholic Theological Union and McCormick Theological Seminary. She is a member of the Ladies of Bethany, a Roman Catholic religious order. She was a participant in the PIP immersion in Brazil in 1991. As a member of Shalom Ministries she served on the LIP Planning Committee and as a mentor.

As teachers and/or mentors in our respective theological and community institutions, we share a commitment to *praxis-based education for transformation.*[2] At its heart is the hope that those of us who are "non-poor" members of seminary communities and churches will learn more about how to minister on the boundaries in ways that promote partnership with and empowerment of the poor,[3] and resist the temptation to exploit the most vulnerable in society for our own institutional or personal advantage.

The commitment to praxis-based education for transformation made Shalom's partnership with the LIP a natural one. Shalom had already established relationships of trust with grassroots leaders— a web of relationships the LIP needed. The LIP offered Shalom members and grassroots leaders opportunities for study and reflection about the systemic changes globalization is bringing to nations and communities. We saw the LIP as a way to challenge our theological institutions to greater partnership with grassroots leaders and communities in addressing the implications of globalization in the communities where our institutions are located.

Our understanding of and commitment to praxis-based education for transformation, and our hope that it can result in cooperation without exploitation, have developed out of our experiences of mission and ministry among oppressed people in, among other places, Chicago, Soweto, Trenton, and the Rosebud and Pine Ridge reservations in South Dakota. Two themes are interwoven in these experiences of ministry, much like warp and woof threads on a weaver's loom.[4]

The first theme is the awareness of how culture, race, class, gender, and other determinants (in short, our social location) shape our ministries. Although much has been written about the ways in which our social location shapes our ecclesial experience and our religious consciousness,[5] the intellectual acknowledgement of difference does not always imply an existential awareness of it. In turn, existential awareness (such as the painful awareness that we are socially privileged in relation to people in our communities) does not always provoke a commitment to change the social structure of our relationships.

Beyond our conscious awareness of the impact of our social location on ministry and mission, the effects of this location on our relationships with the poor are not always visible to us. Like the warp threads on a loom, these background threads are sometimes hidden from view even as we take their presence for granted. We may, for example, acknowledge that we belong to a class that has dominated and exploited the very people with whom we have entered into life and ministry, yet still be unaware of how our interpersonal relationships with the poor are exploitative and demeaning. Even when we are sensitive to both the societal and interpersonal dynamics of power and privilege, the best-intentioned acts of ministry may contribute to the exploitation of oppressed communities because they are embedded in systemic forces more powerful than personal intentionality.

Attending to these warp threads is essential for ministry on the boundaries; without an awareness of how our relationships with the poor are socially structured, our ministries are naive at best and demeaning and destructive at worst.

It is through actual *relationships* with the poor that we are challenged to channel the growing awareness of our place in the structures that shape our lives—the warp threads—from self-preoccupation into action that seeks to confront and to transform those structures. Knowing individuals intimately and sharing in concrete neighborhood struggles for justice can, paradoxically, both wound us and heal us. These relationships are the essential woof threads which give color and life to what we struggle to understand about structures and systems; we are challenged to live differently.

The weaving together of rigorous self-reflection and systemic analysis with the unselfconscious grace in deep friendship is a lifelong art in any relationship. This art is refined and tested through ministry on the boundaries. We are grateful for the rich threads of actual human relationships we have sustained with those socially classified as "the poor," "the oppressed," and "the marginalized." It is through relationships that we learn how people *name themselves* and *name us*. It is through relationships that we are challenged and inspired, judged and shown grace. It is through relationships that we are changed and the patterns of our lives are created.

The accents, colors, and cultures that form the woof of most of the authors' patterns have been gathered world wide, particularly in Africa, Europe, and the United States, among refugees, Native Americans, and African Americans. Each of us recognizes and affirms that the invitation and the attempt to enter into solidarity, vulnerability, and friendship with members of these groups have brought a new unity and wholeness—shalom—to our lives. We will say more about shalom in the pages to come, but here we acknowledge that we have experienced shalom as a gift offered by God through human relationships on the boundaries of our lives and vision.

CHAPTER OVERVIEW

The purpose of this chapter is to share not only the theoretical components of praxis-based education for transformation, but to try to capture something of the drama of this process as it unfolded for us and other participants in the LIP and Shalom Ministries. As readers, you will be invited to imagine the voices of several participants in this process. You will also be offered glimpses of sacred moments in relationships, although we recognize that the printed word cannot completely capture the power of those moments.

We begin with a description of the Shalom mentoring process in the context of the LIP. Following this description we move to an analysis of Shalom Ministries and the guiding vision for its work: the Shalom of God; a discussion of the four guiding theological principles that grow out of this vision of Shalom: mission-in-reverse, development of Base Christian Communities, contextualization, and bridge-building; and a description of praxis-based education for transformation as it is practiced in Shalom Ministries. In our conclusion we return to the hope we expressed at the outset, namely, that there can be cooperation without exploitation in ministry on the boundaries in light of the process we have described.

Members of the LIP who were assigned to Shalom Ministries were invited to explore its vision and principles by volunteering in various ministries: the American Indian Center, the St. Elizabeth Catholic Worker House for homeless mothers and children, the Vietnamese Association tutorial program, the Marjorie Kovler Center for Treatment of Survivors of Torture, and the People's Church ministry with the homeless and residents of SROs (Single Room Occupancy transient hotels).

SHALOM TEAM MENTORING

Six participants of the LIP worked together with Shalom in support of the local grassroots organizations we mentioned in the introduction. Of the six participants, three were students (CTU, CTS, LSTC), two were faculty (MTS, LSTC), and one was a faculty spouse (MTS).

We entered into the immersion project cautiously, but, in consultation with local individuals representing the cultural groups and organizations named above, we agreed that it was a risk worth taking. The leadership of these grassroots groups and organizations expect Shalom volunteers to be culturally and religiously sensitive and to come as those who want to work with and learn from the members of the new culture.

Over the years, Shalom has developed a team approach to mentoring, in which we share responsibility with grassroots mentors and teachers in the groups with which we are associated. This mentoring process depends upon deep levels of trust established in various circles of relationships: between grassroots leaders and local communities, between grassroots leaders and Shalom members, and between Shalom members and local churches, judicatories, seminaries, and schools of ministry.

The trust shared by Shalom members and leaders in grassroots ministries makes it possible for students or church members to make their first entry into grassroots ministries. There is trust that newcomers will be trained to enter into local communities in respectful ways, trained in the principles of Shalom. There is trust that grassroots mentors will help refine and deepen the sincere commitment to ministry that newcomers bring. Thus participants in each community—the grassroots community, the Shalom community, and the various ecclesial communities—continually step out onto an existing bridge of trust. Their behavior in each new encounter can strengthen or weaken that bridge.

Each Shalom volunteer agreed at the start of the LIP to accept supervision and mentoring from both the grassroots and Shalom mentors, and they agreed to attend monthly action/reflection sessions with other Shalom volunteers.

We recognized the delicate balance necessary between action and reflection, particularly as we attempted to enter genuine relationships of dialogue and mutuality with members of groups who are often locked out of power and voice. Without prayer, without serious and honest reflection, our ministry through the LIP ran the risk of "doing good" for others, rather than entering into the project of mutual empowerment. Guided reflection helped us discover our prejudices about the ways members of other social, cultural, and religious groups function in their everyday affairs.

The three-dimensional mentoring process we used provided individuals with many opportunities for reflection.

First, the local grassroots mentors were members of the cultural groups with whom the volunteers worked. They had primary responsibility for introducing the volunteers to all the aspects of the site, including their "assignments." They provided volunteers with insight into the context of the placement, namely, the social, cultural, and religious realities of the people among whom they would be working.

The grassroots mentors became the all-important links for the volunteers with their ability to negotiate the working/learning experience in the new environment. Volunteers were able to engage the grassroots mentors in many specific questions related to culture. These opportunities offered boundary-crossing experiences in which the volunteers found themselves minorities, strangers needing to learn how to live and act within the new social and cultural context.

The grassroots mentors were extremely important as guides and friends, helping volunteers understand appropriate and inappropriate cultural behaviors. They served as interpreters of language, behavior, and meaning who helped bridge the cultural gap between the volunteers and the people among whom they were working. There were occasions when grassroots mentors became close spiritual friends and guides, journeying with volunteers in their continued discovery of God's action in the world through different spiritualities and cultures. One example of this kind of spiritual leadership and friendship can be found in the story of Sam's relationship with Mark in Section 3.

The second level of mentoring involved the Shalom mentors, who had the primary responsibility of helping volunteers reflect on what they were learning in this boundary-crossing experience and guiding a process of personal transformation. Whether in a group or in one-to-one sessions, the volunteers used the four Shalom principles (*See* Section 3 below) to examine what they were learning about themselves, about the attitudes and behaviors they were taking with them into ministry, about how they were changing their assumptions about the people among whom they were working, and about their ability to develop relationships of trust and mutuality with people.

With their Shalom mentors, volunteers could ask their questions, struggle with their doubts, and name their assumptions and prejudices about the people and the contexts in which they were involved. They were given an opportunity to explore, in a safer and more familiar environment, their understandings and misunderstandings of what they were seeing, hearing, and doing. Barbara Blaine, the Director of St. Elizabeth Catholic Worker House, describes how important the relationship with Claude Marie was in her ministry at St. Elizabeth:

> Being in dialogue with Claude Marie has really helped me when my project seemed overwhelming and painful. I am able to get perspective on what my role will be in the future. It is a journey, a process.[6]

As Shalom mentors, we have undergone the same transformative process and have known some of the joys and sufferings of the journey. We tried to be with others as they began to name their own patterns of identity and relationships and identify their goals in mission and ministry. We tried to serve as companions (and sometimes interpreters) in their boundary-crossing experiences. We tried to help them explore how the colors and accents within their newly-developing relationships were affecting who they were and how they understood and practiced mission and ministry.

What we gained in that process was the joy of participating in many holy, transformative moments, as well as in continual challenges to our own patterns of responding to others. In a final interview about her experience with Shalom this past year, a white volunteer said,

> I think there are very subtle ways that an educated person takes advantage. Dialogue asks that we be on an equal footing. I hold power by being white. I have to work very hard to understand how I am present in the African-American community and learn

to listen differently. I can work for change. I have to recognize what a privilege it is to be there.[7]

The struggle to be aware of ways that we "take advantage" is lifelong. As volunteers struggled, we were reminded that our own struggles are far from resolved. But indeed, it was a privilege to be there for LIP participants who entered new experiences of ministry on the boundaries and to embrace the struggle together.

The third dimension of mentoring was the group action/reflection time in which volunteers from all of the Shalom sites met to discuss one of the four principles for mission at each monthly gathering. These occasions of sharing experiences and hearing about the moments of concern and doubt, as well as of joy and success, were enriching for everyone, but these sessions had a more lasting effect than helping each LIP participant realize, "I am not alone in this." They opened windows of greater insight into the process of crossing boundaries as the first step to entering into relationships of mutuality and mutual empowerment. Each participant brought his or her life together with the interpretation of what was happening through interaction with the site context. The reflections of one volunteer, shared in an atmosphere of trust and respect, helped others to articulate their own experiences.

Phyllis and Ted Campbell, LIP participants who worked with Shalom, volunteered to tutor Vietnamese immigrant youth. Toward the end of the school year, one of Ted's students told him that he was reading *The Red Badge of Courage*. At a meeting of the Shalom LIP volunteers, Ted talked about the effort it would take for this young Vietnamese man to understand the key events in that book, taking place during the American Civil War, which would be so familiar to American students. Ted told us that he reread the book himself so he could become his student's "dialogue partner and try to understand his questions as he read."[8]

Those of us who listened to Ted that day saw in this act an example of what it means to practice the Shalom theological principle of mission-in-reverse. Rather than assigning tasks to the student, the tutor did homework himself so he might be more open to the questions that arose from this immigrant student's experience with an American story. The task of reading a book became a shared task, with Ted attempting to follow the lead of the student—not in a passive way, but in an involved and respectful way.

For someone trained to teach and guide (Ted is a seminary professor), it was humbling to learn to follow rather than lead. Ted asked the other volunteers, "How do you get yourself ready for mission-in-reverse? How do you make your first approach not to be in control, not in charge," while at the same time not losing the commitment to contribute your own talents and resources to the relationship? This question is one aspect of the struggle that the non-poor often experience in trying to practice mission-in-reverse.

Thus there was a multidimensional and multilayered quality to Shalom team mentoring. Taken together, they insured that each volunteer was involved in a whole web of relationships and dialogue and was not left to navigate unfamiliar waters alone.

SHALOM MINISTRIES AND THE SHALOM OF GOD

The Shalom vision and spirituality were born in the 1960s in violence-torn South Africa when Claude Marie worked among those oppressed by apartheid and other human rights violations. She accepted the invitation to walk in solidarity with the people of Lesotho and Soweto. This mission required a radicality that could only find its foundation in Christ, the Word Incarnate, and in the trust that God intends unity, wholeness, freedom, healing, and peace for Creation— all that is included in the meaning of the Hebrew word *shalom*.[9] In the following years, with the people of Lesotho and Soweto, in solidarity with people of many cultures, ethnic groups, and religious traditions, the foundations were established for this new ministry.[10]

Today, Shalom Ministries is a worldwide, Christ-centered, covenant community of women and men involved in a ministry of justice, peace, and reconciliation in all parts of the world, including the United States. Shalom members and affiliates covenant before God and each other to live as signs of God's justice with all people. They are committed to living simply among people of different cultures, faiths, and grassroots communities. Part of their work is to educate others for cross-cultural ministries and interfaith dialogue. The headquarters of the community is in Chicago. Since 1975, Chicago-based Shalom members have worked as staff or volunteers in a variety of placements with refugees, in the African-American community, among survivors of torture, and with Native Americans in Chicago and on the Rosebud and Pine Ridge reservations in South Dakota. In recent years, more than fifty ministry students have done their field education at these sites. Claude Marie, Eleanor, and other Shalom members have led thirty traveling seminars on the Rosebud and Pine

Ridge reservations, working in partnership with grassroots Native American leadership. Relationships of trust have developed between several of the cultural groups and a variety of churches and church organizations interested in working with them. Training programs in cultural and mission sensitivity have been offered.

The members of Shalom Ministries and those who volunteer and do field placement with us believe in and hope for the unity and freedom, the wholeness and peace, that is given as promise and challenge in Hebrew and Christian Scriptures, and revealed in the cross and resurrection of Jesus Christ.[11] This hope manifests itself in mission that seeks to be culturally sensitive, ecumenical, open for dialogue,[12] and respectful of our own and the others' religious traditions. This kind of mission is committed to understanding and trust, solidarity and justice, and is based on the self-emptying kenosis to which living as followers of Jesus Christ and his mission calls us.

The unity, freedom, wholeness, and peace expressed in the vision of God's Shalom calls us to accept the consequences of our words about shalom. Our commitment to ecumenism, dialogue, solidarity, justice, and the cross must be a commitment in love and action: a commitment to real relationships with the suffering. True unity requires the vulnerability and openness of those who hold social and economic privilege in these relationships. The Shalom of God becomes the metaphor for what we seek: a way of living that strives to become vulnerable with the vulnerable; to cross over cultural, religious, racial, and class barriers; to enter into relationships of caring and commitment; and to fashion together a way of life that furthers justice and abundant life for all God's people.

SHALOM COVENANT AND THEOLOGICAL PRINCIPLES

The meaning and vision of the Shalom of God informs and guides our Covenant and theological principles:

A. The Shalom Covenant:
   Seeking to live as followers of Christ, we the workers of Shalom will strive to be signs of unity, reconciliation, and healing in a broken world, and to work for justice and peace. When there is division, we seek to be bridges, to carry the burdens of others, sharing concretely in their sufferings, to take risks, never standing still, to be signs of joy and love, to be present and open, ready to

receive as well as to give, freeing us all to become who we are meant to be.

B. The Principles:

   1. *Mission-in-Reverse.* As ministers and missionaries we can and should learn from the people we serve—especially from the poor and marginalized. When ministry is grounded in mutuality and solidarity, ministers become persons immersed in the world of others, like Jesus was in the world of His time. A minister's mission emerges in dialogue with others and is given definite direction as the result of this mutuality.

   2. *Developing Base Christian Communities.* We recognize that the locus of ministry is the grassroots, the base community. We strive to discover and help build community with our teachers—the poor and marginalized. When we meet as a community, we discover a new synthesis of life and faith in Christ.

   3. *Contextualization.* We recognize that fundamental to the proclamation of God's revelation to humanity is the discernment of how God is already present and active in the cultures of the world. We believe in the incarnation of Christ and His redeeming presence in our lives. We recognize that this message must be interpreted, made relevant, by God's people for their own life context.

   4. *Bridge-Building.* We believe in our call to a radical life of reconciliation, which includes engaging with people of diverse cultural, religious, and political backgrounds in building bridges of justice, mutuality, and solidarity.[13]

We will elaborate on each principle and convey something about how Shalom members have encountered them. We will particularly focus on the experiences of LIP participants.

Mission-in-Reverse

Mission-in-reverse means a lack of control in relationships. . . . It is mutual respect. . . . As trust develops people become closer. . . . It is a reversal of the human way of seeing and valuing things. . . . having the mind and desire to be present to each other. . . . It is an attitude of reverence for another person; not just a two-way street of equality, but a reverence of the other person as your teacher. . . . The mystique in mission-in-reverse means being vulnerable . . . to choose to live the kenosis of Jesus who identified completely with the little ones.[14]

"Being with" rather than "doing for" people has been a principle at the heart of the mission-in-reverse idea from its inception.[15] While this is often interpreted in more methodological than theological terms, it has its basis in an *incarnational* model of ministry.

Mission-in-reverse has its theological foundations in the incarnation of God into our world.[16] To believe in the incarnation involves the commitment to be one with the people as Christ was one among us—the willingness, even the desire, to enter into the lives of the poor, the marginalized, and the culturally and religiously "other." It means solidarity in the knowledge that our own wholeness is integrally related to others. It means knowing and accepting the consequences of the solidarity lived by Christ. It means a willingness to empty ourselves in order to enter into the lives of others—their interests, jokes, laughter, and dreams, as well as their pain, danger, repression, and all that diminishes and even destroys their lives.

The hymn in Phil. 2:5–11 ("Make your own mind the mind of Christ Jesus, who . . . emptied himself . . . ") calls us to reflect on the incarnation as God's all-absorbing desire to be united with humankind, a desire that could only be effected by becoming one with us. We encounter a Christ who "did for" others, but from a lowly state, without the negative connotations of "doing for," namely, a condescending, "power over" position. Mission-in-reverse is an acknowledgement of a missionary truth: unity with others requires us authentically to try to enter their world.

Learning to accompany is an essential aspect of ministry on the boundaries. It is a process that takes time, practice, and patience. It almost always starts small, with a listening ear and a "listening heart," as some of our Native American teachers have said, initiated out of respect for what others are thinking and doing. Trust is built through small actions that accumulate over time. Mission-in-reverse is an attitude refined in the tasks, joys, and challenges of everyday life.

One of the goals of mission-in-reverse is true human companionship; there is deep joy to be found there, as well as pain and struggle. Suffering and sacrifice are not the goals of ministry, but, rather, represent the cost of solidarity, what is endured for the sake of the "joy set before us" (Hebrews 12:2) or, as we put it, the vision of God's shalom, which appears not only as future promise but is also realized in partial, fleeting ways in everyday life together.

Developing Base Christian Communities

In recent years it has seemed more and more clear to many Christians that, if the church wants to be faithful to the God of Jesus Christ, it must become aware of itself from underneath, from among the poor of this world: the exploited classes, despised ethnic groups, and marginalized cultures. It must descend into the hell of this world, into communion with the misery, injustice, struggles, and hopes of the wretched of the earth, for "of such is the Kingdom of Heaven."[17]

God's shalom cannot be divided into pieces and distributed as something for individuals and groups to enjoy in isolation. The feeding of the five thousand serves as an example. It was a community event. There was more than enough to eat because everyone participated. No one held back and no one was left out. Jesus took all the available resources, what there was to give, no more and no less. It was more than enough for all.

God's shalom is a community event. For Shalom members, two experiences of community particularly characterize God's Shalom. The first is the spontaneous community that develops among the people with whom we are engaged in ministry, with whom we share daily work, suffering, joy, and prayer. The second is the intentional community that has developed among full members of Shalom Ministries, as we also share work, suffering, joy, and prayer, but with the added benefits of a covenant and a defined process of shared reflection.

An example of the first kind of community is the kind LIP participant Terry Bozich experienced in her placement with mentor George Cairns and the residents of one of the SROs. Terry and George met weekly with members of the SRO for "Friendship Club," which often included Bible study. In an interview with Claude Marie about the year's experiences together, members of the SRO expressed gratitude for the gift of presence and compassion that George and Terry offered. One resident said of Terry, "Miss Terry is really nice . . . she is compassionate." Another resident said,

I don't always join groups. I came to the hotel as a homeless person. I was reluctant to come. I wasn't interested in doing Bible verses. I lost my mother, my father, and husband. Father George just kept coming. He was real nice and quiet and was concerned for the homeless. I just kept coming. Being a one-room occupant, he suggested the Friendship Club (FC). He kept coming. I became interested because he was so compassionate.... He has long patience.

When Claude Marie asked George and Terry what they learned from their friends at the SRO, it was clear that they received from the residents the gift of being included and welcomed among them. Terry said, "It is such a welcoming atmosphere, like coming home." George said, "It is so good to be with you. I've learned so much from the kindness. It is like family."[18]

Community was created out of mutual effort and reaching out from both partners in the Friendship Club, the "seminary people" and the residents. To survive in Uptown Chicago, people need each other. Although there was effort on each side of the partnership ("He kept coming.... I kept coming."), there was also an atmosphere of ease and grace, the "spontaneous community that develops among the people with whom we are engaged in ministry."

The second expression of community, the Shalom covenant community, is inspired by the spirituality of Taizé, Iona, and the U.S. Sojourners. Shalom members have learned from the work of Paulo Freire,[19] Latin American Ecclesial Communities, and other Base Christian Communities in Western industrialized nations.[20] We acknowledge that an essential aspect of community life is defining our identity through prayer and theological reflection together. We identify with the model expressed by James Hug, S.J.: "Reflection on experience understood in light of religious experience by involved communities moving toward conversion and/or action."[21] In monthly reflection meetings, LIP volunteers in Shalom were invited to participate in strenuous reflection on our ministries in a spirit of community.

Contextualization

The development of local theologies depends as much on finding Christ already active in the culture as it does on bringing Christ to the culture. The great respect for culture has a christological basis. It grows out of a belief that the risen Christ's salvific activity in bringing about the kingdom of God is already going on before our arrival.[22]

We believe that God wills for all people the unity and wholeness promised, and that God's love extends to all. Shalom rests in justice, liberation, and salvation for all, and the way we engage in mission and ministry should reflect our belief in God's presence among the people.

We are called to practice listening, respect, and discernment in our relationships with others, in the hope that the incarnate God will become manifest in our relationships. We believe that trust and mutuality will develop through this process so that we can enter into genuine dialogue with the culture and the religious traditions of other people. This process assumes that we are all culturally conditioned, that our ministry takes place with others who are culturally conditioned, that the Hebrew and Christian Scriptures express the revelation of God in culturally-conditioned language and patterns of thought, and that these three cultures are always intertwined in ministry on the boundaries.[23]

Kathleen volunteered at the Marjorie Kovler Center for the Treatment of Survivors of Torture. There she witnessed the efforts of staff and Cambodian women refugees to articulate the experiences of Cambodian refugees. This "bringing to voice" of past experiences of joy and terror and present experiences of struggle and accomplishment could not simply be done verbally—only one of the women spoke enough English to serve as a translator. But the experiences could be acted out; they could be demonstrated through facial expression, through the body, through gestures, through cries and shouts and whispers, through laughter and tears. That is what Kovler staff members Keith Whipple and Patricia Robin and the Cambodian women set out to do, after months of trust-building.

The process of creating a drama through which to tell their story was an arduous one, but the results were powerful. In two public performances, the Cambodian refugees ushered their American audiences into a totally different context, back in time to a world of terror almost beyond comprehension. We were literally invited, through their play, to take their hands and walk through darkened parts of the theater to sit down in a refugee camp and be questioned by a harsh voice that demanded over and over, "What's your name? How many in your family?" We watched as the refugees portrayed themselves as they were years ago, begging for food, being beaten, wondering if today were the day they would die. We were called to understand their struggle to survive and to see what the struggle cost them but gave them.

What Kathleen witnessed at the Kovler Center was the effort to learn, as fully as possible and in ways that transcended words, the stories of these refugees—stories that took enormous courage to tell.

What audacity it would take to "speak" to these refugees without an effort to "hear" their context, not only intellectually, by reading about the Khmer Rouge, but also by "hearing into speech"[24] the experiences that are yet to be given voice, and the truths that lie buried in lonely, painful silence. Only then can true dialogue begin.

Bridge-Building

Basic to the theology of bridge-building is the belief that wholeness and harmony are universal human goals. This shalom is dependent on mutuality and justice among all cultural groups, classes, faiths, races, and sexes. The bridge-builder willingly accepts the role of servant to this goal.[25]

Our pluralistic world challenges us to build bridges between different cultural, class, and religious groups; to help communities develop links with one another; to participate in building a global community; and to celebrate the gifts and challenges of cultural difference.

Relationships strengthened through years of daily ministry and quiet solidarity have taught us that occasions of real dialogue and mutuality do occur on the boundaries between diverse groups of people. Bridge-building is rooted in a theology of reconciliation, one that does not presume that differences can easily be overcome or conflicts neatly resolved by cross-cultural dialogue and relationship, but that commits itself to walk *through* conflict and struggle without abandoning the dialogue or the relationship.

As a LIP Immersion volunteer at the American Indian Center, Mark Thompson wrestled with the history of injustice and violence perpetrated on Native Americans by white Americans. He marveled at the gift of trust and relationship his mentor, Sam Keahna, offered him. Mark's part in building this trust was simply to go to the Center, regularly and quietly, to do whatever needed to be done, to say by presence rather than any grand deed that he desired the relationship itself.

On the boundary, where a new relationship was created, these two people could talk candidly about the nature of their relationship. Mark could express his worry about exploitation, the common pattern in white-Native American relations, and Sam could commission Mark to participate in acts of solidarity that only he, not Mark, could identify as meaningful and valuable to Sam and to his people. The sociocultural power arrangements that place white men in the position of privilege were reversed as Sam said to Mark, "I'm going to ask you to pray at certain times of the day. I'm like your big brother and you are my little brother. We began an everlasting friendship that I hope you will remember."[26]

Through deep relationships created across the boundaries that separate us, a language is created that includes, yet is not confined by, the language of either partner. It is from these relationships that are not relegated to a private sphere but forged amidst the public struggles of our communities that *together* we struggle to give birth to strategies for wider experiences of healing among us.

With these fundamental theological principles of mission-in-reverse, developing Basic Christian Communities, contextualization, and bridge-building clearly in mind, we turn to the process of praxis-based education for transformation as it is practiced in Shalom Ministries.

PRAXIS-BASED EDUCATION FOR TRANSFORMATION

We return briefly to the metaphor of the warp and woof threads that we used in the introduction to this chapter. We spoke of the warp threads as our own primary context and the need to be conscious of the systemic patterns of relationships between the non-poor and the poor. We spoke also of the woof threads as deep personal relationships with the poor, ones that have changed our lives. Personal and social transformation are inextricably bound in human liberation.[27] In the following pages, we will describe how personal transformation and systemic transformation are both nurtured in praxis-based education for transformation.

There is some danger in describing human transformation according to "stages." Human experience is more often a spiral than a linear process. There are always those whose experiences don't follow the prescribed order, and there is an element of surprise that is suggested by the word *transformation*. It conveys more mystery than design.

Nevertheless, we have found it useful to distinguish four identifiable stages in the transformation process: integrating personal life history with ministry experiences, theology, and spirituality; understanding and valuing one's own cultural and religious identity; coming to a more communal and global consciousness and commitment; and becoming involved in co-creating an inclusive, global community committed to justice.

Integrating personal life history with ministry, theology, and spirituality.
This integrative process is essential if the individual is not to risk dis-integration or inability to communicate and be an authentic partner in dialogue.[28] As part of the LIP's process of placing persons in ministry/learning contexts, we encouraged them to reflect on their personal life passages that have preceded their choice and preparation for ministry. LIP participants were given the opportunity to express in the group, or alone with their Shalom mentors, some of their personal history, hopes, call, and goals in preparation for ministry in a cross-cultural context.

Understanding and valuing one's own cultural and religious identity is another integrative step in the transformation process. Going "beyond culture"[29] and arriving at a true respect, acceptance, and ability to communicate with people of another culture requires a healthy un-derstanding and respect for one's own culture and its effects on how one interacts with others.

Shalom members, volunteers, and field education students were not only in cross-cultural contexts, but also ecumenical and interfaith ones. To be able to cross cultural and religious boundaries, we must know who we are but resist imposing our values on others. Intercul-tural relationships require a delicate dance in which all parties, secure in their cultural and religious identities, can communicate with re-spect, openness, and anticipation of something new to be discovered about themselves and others, the creation and the Creator.

Coming to a more communal and global consciousness and commitment is the third stage, in which people "no longer belong only to their own culture—they have participated in the life and world of people from another culture and have been changed."[30] LIP participants were able to experience changes in some of their values, assumptions, preju-dices, attitudes, and behaviors towards people of other cultures and religious traditions. "Entering into the boundary-breaking situation makes it possible for one's worldview to be shifted; perceptions change, so too, the person changes psychologically and spiritually."[31]

Becoming involved in co-creating an inclusive, global community commit-ted to justice is the fourth stage of transformation. LIP ministry con-texts placed us in the midst of people struggling with issues of racism, poverty, homelessness, a high rate of infant mortality, lack of educa-tion and employment opportunities, and cultural, religious, and spiri-tual erosion. It would have required a concrete choice to be unaware of these realities. Participants were challenged to listen and learn from the poor and to become partners with them in the cause of justice and liberation. The Shalom of God cries out for a mission of inclusivity, dialogue, justice; a mission of mutuality and empowerment; a mission of working with, not for; and a mission of personal and systemic conversion toward a world of love and justice.

CONCLUSION–COMING FULL CIRCLE
COOPERATION WITHOUT EXPLOITATION

Through the pages of this chapter we have set out to describe in some detail a process that intends cooperation without exploitation. We have shared the vision and theological principles of a particular venture in cross-cultural mission and ministry, Shalom Ministries. The vision and principles of Shalom chart a particular course through which ministry on the boundaries is to be piloted.

As we recognized in the introduction, the linkage between Shalom Ministries and the LIP seemed a natural one. We share a commitment to prepare future leaders of our churches and theological institutions for ministry and teaching on the boundaries. We want these leaders to understand the systemic realities facing nations and institutions of all kinds—realities most often discussed these days under the rubric of globalization. We desire that our theological schools become increasingly institutionally committed to partnership with grassroots people in the struggle for justice and freedom.

We also want our future religious leaders to learn how to relate in compassionate and empowering ways to the women, men, and children who live on the streets and in SROs, tenements, neighborhoods, impoverished villages, and refugee centers. We want these leaders to be able to build relationships with those whose cultures and religious perspectives are different from their own. We want these leaders to be able not only to talk knowledgeably about global dynamics, but passionately about human beings with whom they have abiding relationships.

Without systemic understanding of the ways our relationships are structured—culturally, politically, economically, socially—our ministries and educational strategies are at risk of being ignorant and naive. Without passionate involvement with human beings despite those structural realities that keep us separated, our ministries and educational strategies are at risk of being distant and passionless—able to talk *about* "the poor" but not *with* them.

The LIP provided an opportunity for the worlds of theological academy and grassroots ministry to engage in deeper dialogue. We believe there has been enrichment on both sides. As members of Shalom Ministries, we have benefited from the discussions of globalization the theological academy has initiated; we have gained a larger view of the world in which we teach and minister. We believe that we have contributed to the partnership a vision of ministry that is eager to wrestle with systemic concerns, and is also deeply rooted in relationship-building on the boundaries.

We said at the outset that it is through relationships that we are challenged and inspired, judged and shown grace; it is through relationships that we are changed and the patterns of our lives created. Our part of the LIP partnership involved facilitating relationships between members of theological communities and members of grassroots ministries and communities, and joining with LIP leadership to mentor the participants in this journey.

As members of Shalom, we also brought to this partnership our own process of mentoring, our vision, our theological principles, and ourselves. Perhaps most of all, we brought our passion for the relationships we have experienced on the boundaries, which have challenged, inspired, judged, graced, and changed our lives. We rejoice in the friendships we watched others forming together with their mentors and with those whom they encountered at their respective sites. We hope that the relationships begun there will have an enduring effect on the pattern of their ministries.

7

Ministry with Persons in Female Prostitution

Depaul Genska, O.F.M.

CONTEXTUAL STATEMENT

I am a priest of the Franciscan Order, and have been actively engaged in ministry with persons in female prostitution since June, 1972. This article is written in conjunction with my mentor, Rev. John Paul Szura, O.S.A., and with Genesis House—a house of hospitality and nurturing for women in prostitution, a site of the Chicago Local Globalization Program. I am on the staff of Catholic Theological Union in Chicago. I am also on the Genesis House board of directors, and volunteer considerable time in promoting Genesis House concerns.

FALLING FROM MY HORSE

It seems that the greatest of life's experiences paradoxically begin with a fall: *the falling* from original creation, *the falling* in love with one another, *the falling* of Paul and others like him from their horses, literally or figuratively. For some, the fall may be both the beginning and, sadly, the end. But for many, a fall is the beginning of new life, in hope, in resurrection! For me, fortunately, the falling off my horse of self-righteousness and pride in my own importance came in the gentleness of a seemingly simple request for a ride.

On a "lazy, hazy, crazy day" of summer heat and humidity, I was driving down Lexington Avenue in New York City. I had come from a going-away party for Linnae and Robert Chickering, a couple whom I had married when I was in parish work. They planned to move from New York City to sunny California. It was a June evening (1972) around 12:30 A.M.

I stopped for a traffic light at the corner of 49th Street and Lexington. Two women, respectably dressed, approached my car as I waited for the light to change. They politely asked, "Sir, would you please give us a ride?"

The only things that crossed my mind were, "They probably do not want to spend money on a cab fare," and, "It is too dangerous for anyone to go by subway at this time of night." I surmised they were only hitchhiking! Appearances can be deceiving.

After some hesitation, thinking they would probably rob me (after all, this was New York City), I responded reluctantly, "OK, please get in the front seat." And they did.

They introduced themselves as Diane Ingram and Jackie Johnson. And I said, "My name is Paul," without any prefix of "Father," a Catholic priest.

Diane and Jackie immediately continued the conversation with, "Well, what hotel do you want to go to?"

I, thinking they were asking only for a ride, said, "Just tell me the hotel where you live and I'll drive you there." They laughed. I didn't think I'd said anything humorous.

Then they asked, "Don't you want to have a little fun before you go home?"

I answered plainly, "Sure—do you want to go to an all-night movie, or bowling?" Where one would go bowling at 12:30 A.M., even in New York City, I hadn't the slightest idea!

Diane and Jackie laughed even more loudly and longer. I don't usually get this good a response from the jokes I tell!

Jackie and Diane judged (long before me, certainly) that I wasn't getting it. They countered, "You don't *get* it, do you?"

Naively, I asked, "What is *it* that I do not get?"

Diane and Jackie stated very matter-of-factly, "We are working women."

Still quite obtuse, I questioned, "Oh, what kind of work do you do? Are you in the medical profession? Are you teachers?"

My reply made them marvel, I am sure, "Two hundred million Americans, and we get *this* one . . . !" And so they had to tell me very plainly, "We are prostitutes!"

I was taken totally off guard. "Gads!" I thought to myself, "How am I ever going to explain this to others—fellow priests, superiors, my MOM?" I do not know how many shades of red there are, but I am sure I must have turned every one of them in split seconds.

Diane and Jackie started back at the beginning, "Don't you want to have a little fun before you go home?"

Now I knew the precise nature of the fun! I assured them as gently as possible (they were being so patient with me), but also very firmly, "No thank you. *That* is against my religion!" Fortunately they took it in good humor and did not press the point, but settled for going for a snack at one of the all-night diners in New York City.

As we three sat eating and talking, I felt quite at ease with them and, I assume, they with me. I told them my profession. "I am a priest, a Catholic priest." At that announcement, they both blessed themselves and admitted they were Catholics. We had something in common!

We stayed at the diner for two or more hours, sharing our lives. They appreciated what I told them and, in no small measure, I was in debt to them for sharing their lives with me.

During the summer of 1972, Diane and Jackie introduced me to several of their friends: other women in prostitution, some customers (johns), and about a half-dozen pimps. It was a revelation of a world I previously knew nothing about. Unless I'd been "knocked off my horse," to this day it would have been a world closed to me and one which, as a priest, I would have condemned.[1]

GENESIS HOUSE

Genesis House[2] is a house of hospitality and nurturing for women in female prostitution. It was providently opened in January, 1984, by Edwina Gateley,[3] a lay missionary from England who came to study at Catholic Theological Union (Chicago). Genesis House is a concrete, compassionate response to the challenge female prostitution presents.

The Genesis House Mission Statement explains:

The Mission of Genesis House is to offer hospitality to all adult women caught up in the system of prostitution, to provide an environment where they can make a free choice regarding their lifestyle, and to assist those who choose to leave prostitution by offering them appropriate services and support.

A primary focus of Genesis House is to provide a long-term

residential program which combines a nurturing, therapeutic, family environment with the necessary support services.

Another important focus of Genesis House is to provide support services and crisis shelter to all women involved in prostitution. Women are made aware of these services through an extensive outreach program.

Genesis House also serves as a voice for change in the political, legal, and social systems which contribute to the perpetuation of prostitution.

Over the years, thousands of women who have been or who are working in prostitution have come for assistance. Genesis House offers help with housing, substance abuse, health care, educational opportunities, parenting skills, legal advice, and numerous other needs. Several of the women leave prostitution and now lead more life-giving lifestyles. Some have not yet left the life-diminishing world of prostitution, but they know they have friends and a safe, non-judgmental place to go when they are ready—Genesis House.

One way to describe what Genesis House offers is to reflect on this acronym: "SHE CARES."

S — "Shes" (and "hes") stand in solidarity with our sisters in prostitution, skillfully assisting them to leave prostitution and lead more healthy lifestyles;

H — Hospitality, with no pejorative judgments allowed; they only serve to further compound the abuse these women in prostitution have already suffered. Perhaps the greatest tragedy that can befall any human being is that everyone has her and his story but either cannot articulate it, or there is no one with whom the story can be shared. Genesis House offers a safe place and listening hearts, where women with a story of prostitution, abuse, and neglect can share their stories to make sense of their lives.

E — Education includes both formal and informal learning to rise above pain inflicted on them by a life of prostitution.

C — Court program takes outreach workers to visit the courts every day, making services and alternatives known to women arrested for prostitution.

A — AIDS outreach program is extensive. Women in prostitution are easily victimized by AIDS and STDs (sexually transmitted diseases).

R — Residential program enables some women to live at Genesis House for long-term assistance. It has been our experience that the longer the women live at Genesis House (one year to one-and-a-half years), the less likely they are to return to prostitution.

E — Empowerment is our goal — to equip the women to do for themselves what needs to be done to live a happy and healthy life.

S — Street outreach provides workers who walk the street where prostitution is practiced to make women aware that Genesis House offers new beginnings and order from chaos.

The acronym is a deceptively simple way to describe the services Genesis House ably provides. The ten-year history of Genesis House proves that while one can briefly describe what Genesis House does, it takes much longer to implement the programs in the lives of women who work in prostitution. It usually takes from two to three years, at a minimum, for an ex-prostitute to leave the close security safety net of the many programs Genesis House offers. When a woman comes to Genesis House, she often needs the services of AA or one of the other twelve-step programs.[4] Often, too, a twelve-step program is not sufficient, so she may need the professional help of a detox center, but these programs are frequently filled to overflowing, and the wait tries one's endurance.

The average woman coming to Genesis House is a victim of incest or other sexual and emotional abuse as a child. Her formal education is spotty at best. She has too few skills to obtain legitimate employment now that the source of her livelihood has ceased because she has quit prostitution. Self-esteem and self-confidence, what little might be left, are all she has. But patiently and perseveringly pursued in cooperation with skilled staff, a genesis happens: a new beginning, order from chaos.

One of the many stories told at Genesis House is "Terry's Tale":

■ *One Friday morning, a policeman saw a pimp chasing a very young and very pregnant girl. It was Terry. She did not want to turn tricks anymore. The policeman arrested the pimp, took Terry to the police station, called Genesis House and begged the counselor, "Do something!"*

Terry shyly came to Genesis House, told her story, ate, took a bath, and went to bed. Her baby was due any day. On Friday evening, two women unexpectedly came for counseling, both in crisis. Jane brought her little ones with her. Jane talked to Ginny (counselor) first. Maggie admitted being suicidal, but she could wait. Ginny's son and girlfriend came to pick up Ginny a little ear-

lier than usual. They were assigned to the task of entertaining Jane's toddlers.

While Ginny and Jane talked, Terry woke up, teetered downstairs and asked Maggie if she knew anything about having babies. Maggie certainly did! Ginny and Jane came downstairs, called the hospital and Terry went off with the paramedics. Jane took over answering the phones, doing crisis intervention while this very human drama unfolded.

The outcome? The suicidal Maggie felt good about herself for the first time in months, having given expert advice on having babies. She thought maybe she did have a reason for living. Jane forgot momentarily what was so important about her crisis, felt she had done a good deed, and took her two kids home to sleep. Sheila, the residential director, returned from an errand and calmed—again—Genesis House. Ginny's son and girlfriend never again wanted to know what happens at Genesis House; they had lived through a typical experience!

New beginings for many people—indeed!

MENTORING INTO A MINISTRY WITH PROSTITUTES

Three people from the Chicago Theological Schools were engaged in the Local Globalization Program (October 1992–May 1993): Dr. Susan Brooks Thistlethwaite (professor of theology at Chicago Theological Seminary), Dr. Dow Edgerton (associate professor of ministry and preaching at CTS), and Ms. Marilyn Olson (student at Lutheran School of Theology). Genesis House staff ably assisted as on-site mentors.

Ms. Sheila Griffin, Residential Program Director, comments,

■ *The interaction in the Chicago Local Globalization Program was an education for all of us: For the students and professors, an enlightenment opposed to society's stereotypical portrayal of persons in prostitution; and for the Genesis House staff and especially the women (former prostitutes)—here were people from the "square" community eager and open to learn first-hand that these women (former prostitutes) are very much indeed beautiful human beings although covered with scars of years of abuse by men, society and even self-imposed disgust with themselves.*
The friendly interaction of the Globalization participants and

the Genesis House community helped tremendously to relieve the years of degradation. The women of Genesis House have loving memories to last a lifetime. The participants made my work easier by the cooperative efforts of Susan, Dow and Marilyn.

I am tremendously well pleased and look forward to future endeavors with the Globalization Program.

CTS faculty member Dow Edgerton looks forward also to continuing the exhilarating and enlightening experience at Genesis House.

- *The experience (at Genesis House) recalled for me some of my earlier roots in public ministry and parish ministry—settlement house work, mental health, etc. Teaching had distanced me from those experiences and the immersion reconnected me. I will continue to work at Genesis House next year, in part because I need to do so.*

You have read of Dow's work at Genesis House, its impact on him, and its relation to the foreign immersions in Chapter 2.

Certainly, for Dow and others who have experienced Genesis House, there comes a new creation for them and those whom they faithfully serve. Many ministerial students have been on the staff and have volunteered at Genesis House during the past nine years—*being with* their sisters who try against many odds to leave prostitution.

Susan Thistlethwaite, another professor, worked in the court advocates' program with an outreach worker as her main mentor. Susan comments:

- *The job of the court advocates is to be a Genesis House presence in several courts in Chicago where women picked up for prostitution-related offenses are arraigned. The Genesis House court advocate talks to the women who are waiting arraignment. In Branch 26 this is done through thick glass, but in Branch 40 we are admitted to the lockup and talk to the women, locked with them in the holding cell, until court appearance.*

  We talk about Genesis House—all of its programs including counseling, health referrals, the residency program, and outreach work. We talk about AIDS transmission, AIDS testing, and living with HIV. We also talk about hepatitis and the rise in tuberculosis and clamydia. We ask if anyone would like a referral to Genesis House and we write down their names. When that woman comes up before the judge, we stand there with her along with the defense attorney and state that she has requested Genesis House. The judges in these courts support the work of Genesis House and will make a referral instead of additional jail time.

Getting to know my on-site mentor has been a key part of this experience for me. After we finished time at the court, she and I would go for coffee and talk about that day in court, or maybe about our kids, or about other things happening in our lives. She got into prostitution by the need to pay college expenses. Her wisdom and matter-of-fact approach to talking to the women in the lockup stems from having "been there" and having gotten out.

The women in the lockup always ask me if I've turned tricks too. I have to say no, though sometimes I offer, "My parents were both alcoholics." They nod—we've shared our pain.

Marilyn Olson, the seminary student, tells of an encounter during her work at Genesis House:

■ On one of my usual Tuesday mornings at GH I went into the kitchen to get some coffee. There were many women there that day, all crowded into the kitchen. All seemed to be talking at once. I got my coffee and after speaking to a couple of the women I knew, I went back to the front reception desk.

As I walked back to the desk, a woman I'd never seen before followed me—through the kitchen, through the dining room, all the way to the front entrance hall. "I said 'Hello' to you two times back there in the kitchen and you never answered me!" she said to me rather angrily.

After I apologized and told her that I'd not realized she'd been talking to me, she accepted my apology. I introduced myself and told her I'd not seen her before. She told me her name and then asked if I worked at GH. "No," I said, "I'm a volunteer."

"Oh!" she said. "One of those rich ladies from the suburbs!" Before I could tell her that she was mistaken, she looked me straight in the eye and said, "Well, that's OK. It doesn't matter what you are. We like you anyway. And you're always welcome here."

I've thought of that incident often. And I've wondered how many of our churches could or would say the same thing to *her.* How many of our seminaries can even begin to teach this kind of hospitality toward the stranger? And isn't that what Christianity is all about? Loving your neighbor. Here, in the form of a drug-

*addicted, scarred, unkempt prostitute, was God's active presence
showing me love, forgiveness, and welcome. I shall long remember and be forever transformed by my experiences at Genesis
House.*

"GOING ON THE STROLL"

Before the mentoring program, in fact since June, 1972, when I first
became engaged in ministry with persons in female prostitution, I
have been taking students "on the stroll"—into the dark city streets
where female prostitution is practiced. There are three components of
"going on the stroll."

1. Preparation: There are several elements needed for the proper
and prudent preparation of those making a stroll. The following are
noted. First, students meet with an experienced street minister to discuss expectations and dispel false notions, and to assure, as far as
possible, that the stroll experience will be one of growth. Second, history and facts of prostitution are outlined. Students are advised con-
cerning the manner of conversation and behavior on the street and in
the bars. Students prepare for entry into a world in which they are
strangers. Yet they will see a world of people much like themselves.
This is the paradox of universal human nature dwelling in different
cultures and expressions, a valuable lesson for ministers and anyone
doing ministry. Third, the dynamics of why prostitution exists and the
connections of prostitution with society and the church are explored.
Some vocabulary is presented, for like theology, this world of prostitution has its own language.

2. The Stroll: The students, prepared to stay out late, leave together
in a group of two or three accompanied by an experienced street minister. They go where prostitution is the customary activity, and pru-
dently engage in talk with both the women (prostitutes) and men (customers) when the occasions present themselves. This is entrance into
an initial friendship—entrance into one another's lives, the minister
and person in prostitution. No immediate revelation of ministry status
is given lest conversation be inhibited. There is simply a meeting of
persons. Repeating such visits brings about a maturing friendship,
one in which the revelation of ministerial status will help and not
hinder the relationship.

3. Theological Reflection: After the stroll, at an acceptable time and
place, the students gather to reflect on their stroll experiences. They

become aware that those who minister with these marginalized people in prostitution have lives that intermingle with and challenge each other.

Some reflections about the exploitation of women in our society and in our churches continually occur. Who has the power in society and in the churches? How is power related to sex? Is the church really all that different from society in general? Are we all prostitutes in some way, selling out in our relationships?

Ministry itself becomes an object of reflection. Students ask what went on that night on the stroll. Some think nothing occurred; others recognize ministerial encounters. The idea of ministry is broadened to include contacts made—person with person, and not just "ministry" as may be narrowly defined in church terms.

One of the astounding experiences of this ministry is that of being ministered to by the very woman who works as a prostitute and who is traditionally thought to be the object of ministry. To grow in awareness that these people have goodness, loyalty, caring, and selfless love is an important step for any minister. There is always the secret temptation to regard oneself as better than someone who works as a prostitute. Sound theology demands a greater humility! There is no evidence that the minister is in grace or that the prostitute is in sin. No one can tell where the corners of sin and selfishness dwell—in the churches or mosques or temples? In the bar? None of the above, or all of the above? Because the mystery of grace cannot be fully appreciated by any human, no one can justify his or her relieved thought, "There but for the grace of God, go I!"

Another ministerial question often posed is whether the church is available in fulfilling its univeral mission of bringing the good news to *all* people. The world seems to read the "signs of the times" more quickly by being available around the clock; police and medical personnel are available all twenty-four hours of each day, and even fast-food places stay open all night! Churches, in contrast, are mainly available only during the day.

This lack of nighttime availability of ministers challenges the kind of ecclesiology operative which restricts ministers, available only for some but not for *all*—day *and* night people!

I often succinctly state my ministry as "priests by day, prostitutes by night; the best of both worlds!" or "ministers by day, the marginalized by night; the best of both worlds!" Certainly the marginalized are present both during the day and night; ministers, just as certainly, are present mainly *only* during the day time. Why?

I quote here only a few comments from some of the over 1600 ministerial students who have "gone on the stroll" in recent years.

Sr. Barbara Jennings, C.S.J.: "There are many impressions that stay with me after making a stroll into the world of female prostitution. My main impression is that the United States is a nation of contradictions; men and women are proclaimed equal in our legal system and church documents, but in practice, there remains very much imbalance. At one of the bars where prostitution is practiced nightly all year round, black women are the objects of white men's prejudice. White men want the black women's bodies; black women need the white men's money. Is it any different elsewhere, where African Americans are still second-class citizens? After all, the laws and pastorals of the churches, the barriers of racial prejudice, coupled with sexual discrimination as in prostitution, persist."

Terry Murphy, ministry student: "I know, as do most of you, that Jesus calls us to accept people for who they are, but that is very difficult in a world—like prostitution—that is caught up with its own rules and oppressions. When I made the stroll, I discovered how I myself am a victim of an exploititive system where it is far easier to label and categorize people into neat little boxes. I did try to be Christlike the night I went on the stroll, but I found myself frustrated with my own powerlessness in not being fully able to accept these people as people struggling to exist with a measure of happiness, but rather looked upon the women as prostitutes and the men as lust-seekers. The experience did show me a world that is often condemned and evokes very little compassion. *I really believe Christ did cross barriers and was able to see persons rather than just label them* for what they do—as tax collectors and prostitutes. I certainly would encourage any interested persons to 'go on the stroll,' but be prepared to be challenged!"

ARE WE ALL PROSTITUTES?

Most people, when that question is asked, are either offended, stunned, or emphatically reply, "No!" Throughout this reflection, that question is implied, but now I ask it forthrightly. It is implied when we realize we are *all* pilgrims in this life, struggling in solidarity to obtain a bit of happiness here and eternal happiness hereafter. The question is implied when I realize I too am a sinner, misusing God's given gifts and talents, and misusing one of the greatest gifts for self-communication with others—the gifts of my sex, sexuality, and sensitivity as a male to other males and females. The question is further implied when, in interaction in friendship and ministry, I secretly or openly behave pharisaically—"Thank God, I am not like this publican." But aren't I like this publican? Am I really without sin of any kind?

Dr. Jean Guy Nadeau, a member of the theological faculty at the University of Montreal, most significantly and eloquently gives a theological grounding for involvement with persons in female prostitution and quite emphatically states that the church really does not have an option to exclude its (the church's) involvement. Dr. Nadeau addressed the Catholic Theological Society of America's (CTSA) Convention in San Francisco in June, 1990 to speak of his years of experience in ministry with persons in female prostitution, in a presentation from his doctoral thesis. I am sincerely most grateful to Jean for his hopeful reflections, and I quote in part from his paper:

> Pastoral practices are at the front of culture, hence of inculturation. Modifying its praxis, a body modifies its self-image, and vice versa. So it is with the Church: modifying its praxis, the Church modifies its ecclesiology, and vice versa. The history of pastoral ministry toward prostitution, in tension between confinement and solidarity, between the virgin Body of Christ and the pilgrim People of God, exemplifies this interaction.

Dr. Nadeau, in his paper, gives a brief outline of the history of former pastoral practice toward persons in prostitution, especially the women. Prostitutes were confined in convents where they did penance for their numerous sins. However, the converted prostitutes were never completely free of the stigma of their past sinful lives. This practice endured through the early- and mid-Christian centuries, and is what Dr. Nadeau calls "a ministry of confinement." He continues:

> New pastoral practices attend to prostitutes not only when they want to change their ways of living, but also when they are still actively practicing prostitution. A shelter founded in the 1940s in Paris, Le Nid, denounced the arbitrary taxation of prostitutes that was added to their juridical repression, and also denounced attempts to confine them anew to brothels. . . . So it was that Le Nid came to play an important role in the strike of the French prostitutes in 1975, and many observers and analysts underlined the fact that prostitutes then turned to, and went to, the Church.

As a matter of fact, many others in society did not want to have anything to do with the prostitutes, fearing ridicule and rejection. . . . [T]he prostitutes went to the Churches and even occupied them . . . because the Church had already gone to them, because some Christians and ministers already supported their cause.

Bishop Cadilhac, on behalf of the French Episcopal Council for the Working World, emphasizes the subjectivity of prostitutes as human beings: "We can only act *with* prostitute persons and not *for* them. They must be subjects, the authors of their own liberation and of the liberation of their world, learning to walk by themselves, discovering their dignity and self-confidence. Otherwise, we substitute our answers for their own and, instead of helping them, we alienate them further. *With them* we become founders of the Church."[5]

MINISTRY EDUCATIONAL CONTRIBUTIONS

Enumerated here are five ministerial educational contributions provided by the challenge of ministering with persons in female prostitution.

1. Respect for the dignity of persons. A central emphasis motivating church renewal is respect for the dignity of all persons. This may remain a theory in the classroom, but insight comes alive when students encounter those whom society has little reason to value other than for their personhood. A constant temptation is to value *the other* for conditions and circumstances having little to do with the core of his or her person. When a student gets to know, understand, appreciate, and even love persons in prostitution for *the persons they are*, the deep mystery of personhood and its dignity are bases for life and not mere church documents.

What life is all about is relationships. As Chapter 6, "Ministry on the Boundaries," puts it so well,

. . . it is through relationships that we are challenged and inspired, judged and shown grace; it is through relationships that we are changed, and the patterns of our lives created.

2. The mission of the Church is to preach the gospel to the poor. Few groups are as marginalized as persons in female prostitution.

When they are victims they are treated like criminals. When they are with other men or women they seem not to fit in. Even when they are with "their own" there is often competition and jealousy preventing real acceptance and friendship. To reach out to these people is to reach out to a group marginalized, more often than not, both by society and by the churches.

How does one reach out to the poor and marginalized so as not to further marginalize or exploit them? The essential principle is often simply called "mission-in-reverse," but in practice it is not so easily accomplished.

Learning to accompany is an essential aspect of ministry on the boundaries. It is a process that takes time, practice, and patience. It almost always starts small, with a listening ear [or with gestures of interest,] initiated out of respect for what others are thinking and doing. Trust is built through small actions that accumulate over time. Mission-in-reverse is an attitude refined in the tasks, joys, and challenges of everyday life. (*See* Chapter 6, "Ministries on the Boundaries.")

3. The imitation of Christ. In professional education for ministry, there is often a neglect simply to imitate Christ as a guiding norm. In the hurried preparation of techniques and knowledge, the student may not be urged strongly enough to do what Christ did and to go where Christ went. This ministry is a constant and unforgettable challenge to keep Christ's example uppermost. (*See* Chapter 8, "A Matter of Homelessness.")

4. Person and system. Ministry sometimes relates well to individuals but neglects the systemic issues. Frequently the reverse is true. It is difficult to be present with persons in female prostitution for long enough to forget either person or system. The person is always the key factor, encountered in pain, boredom, difficulty, need. The total reality is the constant evidence of a system of social relations, laws, expectations, and other factors that make the person what he or she is. One cannot be with persons in prostitution without making a serious critique of society and systems. However, even in the hard-headed critique, the individual is always present.

5. Local and global dimensions. Prostitution is often referred to as "the world's oldest profession." It is certainly older than Christianity! Every culture has its forms of prostitution, in Africa, the Americas,

Asia, and Europe, every city includes the "lively commerce" of prostitution.[6]

Conservatively estimated, there are over 100 million persons engaged in female prostitution. This counts both the women (prostitutes/madams) and the men (customers/pimps). For every woman, there are ten to fifteen men. Certainly the men have to be counted—women do not prostitute by themselves![7]

Instead of calling this global phenomenon female prostitution, it should be called "heterosexual" prostitution since both men and women are necessary to its existence.

Time magazine featured the cover story, "Sex for Sale: An Alarming Boom in Prostitution Debases the Women and Children of the World."[8] It is worth reading, not just because it is interesting, but also as a lesson for ministers who might mistakenly think that prostitution is an esoteric concern of the few. Prostitution is "alive" but not "well" for the millions of people worldwide who are engaged in it.

We have contacts with 247 ministers in 29 countries throughout the world who minister to persons in female prostitution. The harvest, however, always remains greater than the laborers. If anyone reading this knows of ministers working with persons in female prostitution, we would appreciate our name and address being given to them, and theirs to us, so we may share insights and inspiration from one another.[9]

In using female prostitution as a paradigm for theological study, the English alphabet includes abuses (physical/emotional/sexual), addictions, AIDS, battle of the sexes, criminal justice system, cross-cultural discrimination, drugs, education and empowerment, feminism, higher power/self-help support groups, few laborers, harvest, multiple ministerial challenges, poverty, and prejudice.

The question is simple. "Faced with the challenges presented by the pervasiveness of prostitution, how do we respond?" The answer is not as simple. Matters of relationships, sexuality, spirituality, STDs, violence, and a wide range of women's issues complete the alphabetization challenging the zeal for the Lord's people.

PILGRIM OR TOURIST?

Dr. Doris Donnelly, associate professor of theology at John Carroll University in Cleveland, Ohio, in her article "Pilgrims and Tourists:

Conflicting Metaphors for the Christian Journey to God," provides a significant elucidation on ministerial evolvement.[10]

Adapting Dr. Donnelly's insights and applying them in this ministerial context, we ask a most serious question: Are we involved as pilgrims or tourists? This difference is the *whole* difference!

Dr. Donnelly states there are five basic ingredients to being a pilgrim as opposed to a tourist. First, pilgrims perceive an internal dimension to pilgrimage; tourists are concerned with the external only. Depth, not distance, is the goal for the pilgrim, but not for the tourist.

Second, pilgrims invest themselves; tourists avoid personal commitment. Investment of time, talent, and treasure by the pilgrim yields ample dividends and profound insights; for the tourist, there is hardly any investment of anything worthwhile or enduring.

Third, the focus for the pilgrim is to be affected by the pilgrimage; the tourist seeks to be untouched at all.

Fourth, both the journey and the arrival are of import for the pilgrim; only the arrival matters for the tourist. The Emmaus story perhaps best illustrates this; the journey itself is the occasion for growth in loving recognition that the stranger is actually Christ in disguise. At the arrival, with the generous offer of hospitality, the disguise evaporates and the inner blindness of wayfarers yields to sight and celebration.

Finally, community is formed for the pilgrim; community is unimportant for the tourist. For pilgrims bonding with those with whom one makes the pilgrimage is essential—we are all connected! Pilgrims are also in solidarity with those visited on pilgrimage. There are two ways among the many in which persons in female prostitution are directly encountered in pilgrimage: "going on the stroll" and Genesis House—a place of hospitality and nurturing for women in prostitution. "Going on the stroll" into the city streets where female prostitution is practiced offers serious pilgrims the opportunity to see firsthand some of the "problems" of prostitution. More importantly, "going on the stroll" puts human faces on the people who, for whatever reasons, are there practicing it.

As a means of continuing our process of being involved with the marginalized in prostitution, the following are suggested for implementation:

Personally:

1. I promise to take the phenomenon of female prostitution seriously, realizing that globally over 100 million persons are presently engaged in it.

2. I will read at least one book on female prostitution in the next six months; and I will view and analyze one film about female prostitution in the next six months.
3. I will initiate and maintain a friendship with a woman or man engaged in female prostitution.

Professionally:

1. I plan to discuss the phenomenon of female prostitution with my colleagues within the next six months.
2. I plan to develop a strategy to educate myself and my colleagues about female prostitution.
3. I will analyze the relevant implications of female prostitution and its local and international impact on society.

Pedagogically:

1. I plan to do serious research on female prostitution history— its development throughout the centuries, people involved, etc.
2. I plan to use more examples in my teaching and lecturing from the world of female prostitution.
3. I plan to be in contact with others who are knowledgeable of the phenomenon of female prostitution.

Pastorally:

1. I plan to volunteer at an agency or ministerial site which works with persons in female prostitution.
2. I plan to introduce other ministerial colleagues into the often ministerially neglected world of female prostitution.
3. I will examine my own attitudes and actions to eliminate any prostituting thoughts, words, or behaviors I might have.

In these ways, we learn to move from apathy to appreciation to action in love concretely enfleshing the ministerial skills this book offers to the phenomenon of female prostitution, a phenomenon which presents innumerable ministerial challenges. In these ways, the hopeful words of Ephesians 2:19 are fulfilled in our time:—"We are strangers and aliens no longer" but friends, companions in our pilgrimage in this life.

8

A Matter of Homelessness

Anthony J. Gittins, C.S.Sp.

CONTEXTUAL STATEMENT

I am originally from England and am a member of the Congregation of the Holy Ghost, a Catholic missionary order. A "resident alien" in the United States, I am currently professor of theological anthropology at the Catholic Theological Union in Chicago. After training in anthropology and linguistics at the University of Edinburgh, for much of the 1970s I was stationed in Sierra Leone, West Africa, working with village communities.

The relationship between Christian theology and Christian discipleship is one of my major preoccupations. Because authentic theological discourse is not confined to the classroom or library, I feel challenged to seek it elsewhere. This has led to my continuing attempt to engage with people on the margins of society, people whose voices are not commonly heard in theological circles. The substance of this chapter is the result of almost a decade of very "low-key" ministry (ministry: "attending to") in a shelter for homeless women, where body language is as informative as the mother tongue.

"Mission-in-reverse" is increasingly understood as "attending to" people in such a way that their words and actions help generate dialogue and incipient friendship. It is a delicate undertaking, particularly among those who commonly perceive themselves as insignificant in the world of "respectable" people around them. But since this perception is the very one Jesus encountered throughout His own ministry it should, if attended to, yield a harvest of insights for anyone who ventures into our cities in the footsteps of Jesus.

"The poor are not our problem: we are theirs." This lapidary saying contains much hidden wisdom. Working among the poor seems
to have provided access to some of this wisdom. And since wisdom
is not private property, it is offered to any who come across this
chapter.

A SHELTER FOR HOMELESS WOMEN

Chicago's "Uptown" neighborhood belies its upbeat name. In an
area approximately one mile wide and two miles long there are
people of a hundred nationalities. Uptown is home to 144,000 people,
which is ironic, because that is the number of the elect: "the people
who have been through the great persecution; . . . they will never hunger or thirst again; . . . and God will wipe away all tears from their
eyes" (Rev. 7:4, 14–17). It is reliably estimated that there are some
50,000 homeless persons in Chicago. In the basement of People's
Church, threescore and more men are offered a bed and a meager
meal every night between October and May, while a few blocks away,
in the basement of the Uptown Baptist Church, up to forty women
are offered similar hospitality.

Shelters rely heavily on volunteers, and participants in the "Local
Immersion" component of the Chicago Program for Globalization in
Theological Education served in this capacity. Thus they attempted to
merge into an existential reality (the women's shelter and its activity)
which existed long before they came and which would continue long
after they departed, yet which may never even have adverted to their
passing through. So what is the value of such "volunteerism"? How
might it be undertaken to greatest effect and how would such effect
be gauged? And in what sense, if any, could such "low-profile"—and
transitory—presence be justified as Christian ministry?

"It all depends what you mean by . . ." is a familiar qualifier for any
overly simplistic judgment. When attempting to judge the value of
something as nonspecific as the activity of volunteers in a shelter,
many qualifications and caveats will be necessary. But there is a particular approach, borrowed from the social sciences and applicable to
theological education, which may be uniquely valuable to at least
some people, and by means of which it might be possible to ensure

that "mere volunteerism" might be transformed into authentic human encounter.

The existential reality of homelessness in Chicago provided one of the sites for those people in theological education wishing to take advantage of an attenuated "immersion experience." Wary of the cruder manifestations of "volunteerism," wherein patent "outsiders" foist themselves on hapless "insiders" in a more or less ostentatious and self-conscious attempt to "help," the organizers of the current phase of the Globalization of Theological Education attempted a rather more subtle approach. It was deemed appropriate to gather under the aegis of one of the Chicago shelters in which there were experienced staff persons as well as an ongoing involvement by people engaged in theological education for ministry.

Into this core group were gathered, as gently as possible for all concerned, the members of the Local Immersion Group. One night, the first of the two was introduced to the shelter by me as mentor. A week later, and in a similar manner, the second was introduced, teaming up with a different group of volunteers, but accompanied again by me in my role as mentor. In subsequent weeks each or both of the pair would spend a night at the shelter, rotating with other volunteers, either with or without the mentor on any particular night. The rationale is as follows.

It seemed important to introduce the new participants only one at a time, both so that they could be monitored and attended to, and so the women guests of the shelter might better gain their acquaintance. Before each of them came for the first time, the mentor provided some simple introduction to the shelter and its procedures. There seemed little point in an elaborate introduction when actual engagement with the reality of the shelter was to be a central part of the process. Consequently, a minimum of data was provided: simple statistics, a description of the shelter, and the duties of volunteers. It was made clear that "participant observation" would be the major means of fact-finding and accommodation to the group of homeless women, though the nature of participant observation itself was not exhaustively explained.

From 9:30 P.M. until 7:00 A.M. the following day, the volunteer is at the shelter, preparing and serving food, checking lists of incoming guests, schedules for showers, cot allocations, and providing towels and toiletries. A meal is served at 10:00 P.M., and by 11:00 P.M. lights are out and the volunteers may sleep until 5:45 A.M., with a minimum of disturbance. Breakfast is cooked and served, the shelter is cleaned, cots are removed, and everyone, including volunteers, is back on to the bustling streets at 7:00 A.M. The volunteers are provided with ample opportunity to observe and participate.

Initially, some volunteers are, understandably, bemused, self-conscious, challenged, and subject to a variety of new feelings and sensations. Some appear to withdraw from social contact, busying themselves about their "chores" and not participating much in the give and take of the shelter. Others, more exuberant, comfortable, or risk-taking, throw themselves into the unfamiliar situation with gentle availability or naive commitment. The balance between participation and observation cannot be achieved by one person alone; it is the fruit of relationship. And relationships take time to build, especially between middle-class whites and bruised and broken homeless women, mostly Hispanic and African-American.

PARTICIPANT OBSERVATION AND ANTHROPOLOGY

Bronislaw Malinowski, an expatriate Pole working in the Trobriand Islands to the southeast of Papua, New Guinea during the Great War (1914–1918), was interned there for the duration. Making a virtue out of necessity, Malinowski attempted an "in-depth" study of the Trobrianders, eventually producing a series of scholarly potboilers with titles like "Sex and Repression in Savage Society," and establishing his reputation as an anthropologist of prodigious and exotic learning. He also canonized "participant observation" for subsequent generations of fledgling anthropologists committed to understanding the "other," from the rain forests to the tundra, and from Alaska to Zimbabwe.

As a so-called human science, anthropology and its methodologies do not always meet with the unqualified approval of the "hard" sciences, interested as they are in experimentation, systematization, replication, and generalization. But human agents—people, whether individually or in groups—are not amenable to the same control or treatment as are the data of hard science. People are predictably unpredictable, and often idiosyncratic in their actions, reactions, rationales, and explanations.

Participant observation, refined over the course of the twentieth century, stands as an unapologetic adaptation of the "hard" scientific experimental method to the realities of human life. It is thus a compromise between reducing people to ciphers, and admitting that free will effectively places human behavior beyond the explanatory and predictive reach of authentic scientific inquiry. Participant observation, properly understood, is proposed by anthropology as the most appropriate and, indeed, effective way to comprehend the dynamics of the everyday life of people. And, while having at least some of the virtues of scientific inquiry, it is also perceived both as an art form and as a way of life.[1]

The challenge of participant observation. Perhaps the greatest challenge to anyone who attempts to understand other people's behavior and the rationale of belief underlying it is to "let go," to relinquish control, to surrender the initiative, to let the other person "be." Unless this challenge is met, almost all the data collected about others will be contaminated and all the conclusions will be spurious, for what will have been observed will not be "normal" or "typical" behavior, but behavior significantly modified by the presence and effect of the observer. The observer, of course, will be quite unaware of this. Writing of the experience of participant observation, one author uses the word "immerse"; one must immerse oneself as thoroughly as possible in the community being studied.[2] The word is apposite, for one must try to contextualize oneself in the very same medium as that experienced by the "insider," a daunting task. Immersion is far from being a mere "dip," or even a "plunge." Those are short-lived or superficial episodes; immersion is a total experience. Activity comparable to a dip or a plunge is not authentic participant observation. The latter takes considerable time, real commitment, and requires vulnerability.

Furthermore, if people's behavior is constantly monitored and modified in the presence of the "outsider," how can any outsider really understand the dynamics of what, for the insiders, constitutes the reality of everyday life? "Only by at least some participation in community life can [the outsider] hope to understand what people really think and how they really act, which are not always the same as what they say they think and how they say they act, when they are asked."[3]

The fruit of participant observation. If one can, to some degree at least, become "immersed" in the ongoing life of others, then one of the first fruits of such an experience is the ability to interpret, to make some sense of that life, not simply from one's own logic or inference, but according to the point of view of those for whom this constitutes daily reality. The participant-observer will be able to refine his or her initial inquiries, moving from a simple "what happens?" to a more nuanced set of questions:

—What do I think is happening?
—What do the people think is happening?

—What do I think about what is happening?
—What do the people think about what is happening?
—What do I think should happen?
—What do the people think should happen?[4]

With an expanded list of questions such as these, it becomes possible to perceive both the gap between one's own interpretation and assessment and that of others, and in any subsequent movement from the typical "outsider" point of view to that of the "insider."

Central to any culture or subculture is the existence of shared meanings, values, and common understandings. In fact, these give identity to a group and also mark it off from other groups. One of the sweetest fruits of participant observation is its harvest of insight into other worlds of meaning. Only by having access to other people's point of view is this possible in principle. Mere participation or observation according to the outsider's criteria is insufficient to yield access to other people's point of view; that demands many other qualities in the participant-observer. But the method does lend itself to the acquisition of "unique pictures of an alien and unfamiliar world view: the perspective, the social dynamics, or the central and sometimes secret moralities of a culture."[5]

This is not to say, however, that meaning is reducible to those things which the agents or actors can articulate; it is perfectly possible to uncover very clear and compelling patterns of meaning, of which "insiders" are quite unconscious. The challenge to the interpreter is to seek out the *many* levels of meaning rather than to impose a single one as an absolute, or to accept the insiders' explanations as definitive and exhaustive.

Successful participant observation. Participant observation, as the name suggests, is an undertaking in which there is interaction between an "outsider" and persons whom we might speak of as "insiders." But it is interactive in another way; it attempts to study, and to make sense of, interactive meaningful behavior specifically as perceived and experienced by the insiders themselves. Such a methodology is most effectively pursued when access to the subject matter of research can be gained through access to the experience of people's daily lives—when, to a significant degree, the actual topic of research *is* people's daily experience. This presupposes that the researcher be either an "insider," a perspective virtually impossible for any "outsider" to achieve, no matter how long associated with the "in" group, or at least be granted a position of privilege relative to insiders and their daily experience.

A research topic, however, must not simply be coextensive with people's daily life, but must be rather more tightly focused lest it become quite diffuse and unmanageable.[6] Thus, one should not imagine that "homelessness" can be adequately researched; rather, "these particular homeless people" may be one's primary focus, with perhaps another group, or even another piece of research, providing a comparative base.

Clearly, the inquirer must have the minimum tools for gathering and interpreting information: language, comparative data, or a template or model against which information can be matched and gauged. Since much of the information is provided in the words, images, and body language of the "insider," a certain linguistic and metalinguistic proficiency is demanded of the participant-observer. And because interpretation is a goal, there is need—for the maximum value of the undertaking—for at least a minimum of alternative scenarios, not only for comparative purposes but also to help minimize generalizations arising from too narrow a base of knowledge. The participant-observer must constantly keep in mind that social meanings are *relative*, to both context and person, and that the more one can fill in the background against which a particular experience can be foregrounded, the more persuasive will be the provisional interpretations.

Procedurally, of course, the inquiring participant-observer may indeed identify a general issue, such as "homelessness." Moving between the general and the particular, the inquirer will attempt to become informed about the overall ("macrocosmic") issue of homelessness, while attempting to identify a particular manifestation ("microcosmic"). It is this latter which becomes the focus of attention, and the study of which both produces new information and modifies the understanding of the macrocosmic problem. The critical characteristic of participant observation, however, is that "[the] concepts are derived from the meanings people use to make sense of their daily lives. In other words, concepts are defined phenomenologically."[7] Yet this does not absolve the observer from a critical assessment of what is happening.

Perhaps the social drama as studied by participant observation, whether it be homelessness or something else, will yield information that in some way illuminates other information generally available through objective data-gathering; or perhaps it will not. The intention is not to replicate other findings, whether statistical or behavioral, but precisely to produce an "insider's" perspective, having some verisimilitude, which is then interpreted or translated for other publics. Such a perspective is deemed to be inherently significant and valuable.

CONVERSION, RESOCIALIZATION, AND CHRISTIAN MINISTRY

Anthropologist Michael Jackson, in a study of the Kuranko people of Sierra Leone, West Africa, adopted a form of participant observation he called "radical empiricism."[8] Medievalist Carolyn Walker Bynum has spoken of Christian conversion in terms of "radical disjunction" and "radical continuity."[9] The common element is "radical." Jackson avers that only by a radical entering into the daily reality of other people's lives can one claim any degree of self-actualization or authentic insight—a point which could translate very well into the lives of Christian ministers. In rather similar vein, Bynum argues that a person can indeed be reintegrated in a very fundamental way, without being first disintegrated. For some people, it is true, religious conversion is experienced as disjunction, a severing of some of one's past and a redirecting of one's energies and goals. But for others, Bynum identifies conversion as more of a continuity, a reengagement and recommitment to the future as an extension of the past and present. But whether by disjunction or continuity, the Christian is surely called to follow Jesus on the Way (Mark 10:52).

Participant observation may help people of faith by providing an authentic opportunity, not only for our learning about other people's perspectives, but for engaging with their lives in such a way as to have our own radically transformed. And this, it would seem, is an expression of our own conversion, whether or not it results in the conversion of others.

"Resocialization" is the process described in one's personal appropriation and transformation of the educative or socializing processes through which one becames a member of a social group—an insider.[10] By adolescence, I may well understand objectively what parents, the law, or God expect of me, but I must go further and assimilate or "own" a certain way of being in the world by making a synthesis of these and other expectations, which will form the basis of my future actions and judgments. This synthesis is not so much an objective reality as is the actual process of resocialization, a process that may last as long as my life lasts.

No one actively and sensitively meeting the radical challenge of participant observation will emerge unaffected, unscathed. The quality and validity of the information and insights gained depend intrinsically on the quality of the relationships built and sustained by outsiders and insiders. Because participant observation engages the researcher with other people and with their experiences and interpretations of daily life, it implies that the researcher be caught up in an educative process of socialization, or, more accurately, since it is not the process of creating an initial, enduring world, resocialization. In theological terminology, this can be seen as "conversion" if it means the turning away from what does not lead to God and the turning toward what appears more Godly. Potentially, therefore, participant observation is an instrument of grace. Potentially, those whom one reaches through participant observation are the mediators of that grace. Therefore those who undertake participant observation for the sake of the Kingdom must be prepared, to paraphrase Max Warren, to take off their shoes, for they are on holy ground.

MENTORING AND PARTICIPANT OBSERVATION

Participant observation is not simply a means to an end; it is, we might almost say, an end in itself, which should not be assessed only "objectively" or in terms of what data it produces, but which should be perceived as intrinsically valuable as a way of being in the world, a world of and a world with others. Of course, the same may be said of ministry itself. The minister must acquire a *habitus* or attitude; participant observation, begotten in the social sciences but born in our daily lives, can justly characterize the pastoral *habitus*. Let us examine its constituents more closely.

The participant-observer acknowledges that cooperation and trust are the most authentic ways to promote human understanding, and that learned respect for the other is a sign of affirmation. Those who approach others with these dispositions are more likely also to learn how to operate meaningfully and appropriately in an unfamiliar cultural situation. Cannot the minister do likewise?

Participant observation is not a technique to be learned for specific interactions, but a fundamental modification of mentality and behavior which depends not on the mastery of a series of steps, but upon finesse, patience, respect, the lack of pomposity and dogmatism, and integrity. Such qualities are not easily learned or assimilated, which partially explains why participant observation is a lengthy process built on mistakes, apologies, and new starts. Is not this also true of ministry? But while participant observation is capable of bringing out the very best in a minister, it is no simple matter, and will frustrate and defeat the inflexible, the condescending, and the judgmental.

Those who wish to control initiatives, to dictate "should" and "ought," to cry "sin" and "wicked" too readily, will not find participant observation congenial. It requires that one become caught up in other people's lives as a participant, in ways that range from the peripheral to the central. But only those *really* interested in the other as a whole person—not simply as "homeless," "woman," or perhaps even "outcast" or "sinner"—will capitalize on the potentialities of participant observation. *real* interest in another person leads us to relate to that other as subject and not merely as object; and that should lead to empathy, which in turn produces a modification in one's own agenda and response—and the cycle continues.

In the kind of interaction described here, the initiative does not rest with the researcher or minister; it rests significantly with the "insiders" who will call one to engage in a number of different relationships and roles, which may range from the uncongenial to the unacceptable. The greatest challenges will be to retain one's integrity while maintaining the interest and rapport of the other person or a whole group, to push the limits of one's customary behavior without fatally compromising one's identity, and to learn when to demur and even resist external pressures or expectations.

If ministry is about "attending to" others and "serving" their needs, then how can this be effected among people whom we do not understand, and whose lives are hugely different from our own? Participant observation is a way of gaining entry into other people's lives: a way that is neither aggressive nor manipulative. Insofar as it is successful it will afford the possibility of and opportunity for honest Christian ministry, and not only of a one-sided kind, of it nature it involves mutuality, relationality, and reciprocity.

Some well-intentioned participant-observers in fact remain rather sidelined, while others are readily assimilated into the group they encounter (which, as we noted, does not mean they become insiders). The more effective ones manage to strike a balance between being outsider and being insider, being unchallenged and being overwhelmed; in large measure this depends on the degree of mutuality extablished. All of the above may be equally true of the minister. As always, Jesus serves as example, as challenge, and as hope.

THEOLOGICAL METHOD, MINISTRY, AND HOMELESSNESS

There is a fine line between attachment to or empathy with an unfamiliar group and identification of or absorption into it. All Christian ministers worth their salt will be compassionate toward the outcast, the marginalized, the "sinner," but the call to ministry is not a call to *become* a prostitute or a felon or a homeless person. What is one to do? Jesus neither compromised himself nor avoided others. He did not become a tax collector or sinner, but became a "friend" of such persons. He also "did not cling to his [divine status] but emptied himself . . . and became as [human beings] are" (Phil. 2:6–7). A careful consideration of exactly how he accomplished this discloses a quintessential example of what we have seen as participant observation, an example manifest in the lives of Christian ministers from Augustine to Luther, and from Damian of Molokai to Mother Teresa of Calcutta, people whose fundamental integrity is unquestionable.

"The poor are not our problem; we are theirs." This epigram effectively stimulates a novel perspective. Jesus was preeminently able to identify the problem of the poor *from their own perspective,* and by doing so liberate them in such a way that they could effectively be healed or help themselves. Yet by no stretch of the imagination was Jesus a member of the social category of "the poor" or "the sinner." So long as we, in our turn, fail to identify the problems of "the poor," or identify them only in our own terms, to that degree we will fail to build bridges or part waters, thus allowing their exodus to the Promised Land.

In the abstract, or from the perspective of a comfortable armchair, "homelessness" may be judged to be a human tragedy, a socially sinful condition, a rich pastoral opportunity, or all of these and more. Whether from the armchair or, indeed, from the shelter itself, ministers may not be able to foresee a "solution" to the "problem." But any minister whose theology is not being tested in the fire of experience, and any minister who is a stranger to the experience of human deprivation and suffering, albeit often in rather vicarious forms, is not credibly engaged with the human community he or she purports to serve.

Jesus assumed the condition of a slave (Phil. 2:7) as he reached out to those enslaved in body or spirit. As followers and ministers we need to learn to do something similar. Unfortunately, by dint of privilege and even by grace, we are greatly removed from some of the most needy members of society. Unfortunately, not only do we often fail to hear the cries of the poor, but we may also fail to be instructed by their own theology and their own experience of God, of justice, of the church, and of Christians.

Jesus paints a sobering picture of the Last Judgment, when people will be judged, not by their formal piety or religious affiliations, but by their response and sensitivity to the needy. He stands before us with the stark challenge of his incarnation:

> "I was hungry, and you . . . [?];
> I was thirsty, and you . . . [?];
> I was a stranger [. . .], naked [. . .], sick [. . .],
> in prison [. . .], and you . . . [?]"
> Matt. 25:35–36

Participant observation is a modest attempt to situate us "where the action is." If effective, it will change our perspectives. If effective, it will be because we have learned to listen and respond. If effective, it will mean that the agenda of—in this instance—the homeless has become part of our agenda. And so, personal conversion in the minister, attentiveness to the community as theological resource, and the modification of the theological agenda itself will have been effected.

PART III

THEOLOGICAL AND PEDAGOGICAL REFLECTIONS

9

Theological Reflection in the Community Based Model

Yoshiro Ishida

CONTEXTUAL STATEMENT

My involvement in the Globalization of Theological Education (GTE) began over one year before our participation in the Plowshares Pilot Immersion Project for GTE (PIP/GTE). When I joined the Lutheran School of Theology at Chicago as the director of its Center for Global Mission in 1989, I was made aware that some colleagues in Hyde Park already had been very much involved in the GTE for several years. Thus our efforts for the GTE were not initiated by the Plowshares Project which, nevertheless, has become an occasion for us to enhance our joint efforts for the GTE in Hyde Park. The Hyde Park Cluster, therefore, while applying for PIP/GTE, placed an emphasis on the significance of a *joint* venture by stating, "The chief reason we urge the serious consideration of this joint application . . . is the possibility it gives to relate the globalization goal to *ecumenical cooperation* as well as *curricular innovation* in theological education." We anticipated that a shared intensive immersion period would multiply the impact of the project on the ethos of the cooperating institutions. I served as the overall coordinator for the PIP/GTE for the initial period of 1988–1989, and continued to function as the coordinator of the Lutheran School of Theology at Chicago for the PIP/GTE of the Hyde Park Cluster.

The Local Immersion Project in Chicago, which took place in September, 1992–May, 1993, in conjunction with the PIP/GTE, was designed with the following specific features: First, the Chicago context, with a large number of seminaries clustered geographically, provided unique opportunities and challenges. Second, the community based educational programs, such as the Chicago Center for Public Ministry, Shalom Ministries, Seminary Consortium on Urban Pastoral Education, were chosen as the sites as well as the contexts for the Immersion Project and their program directors were represented on the planning, coordinating, and evaluation team. Third, the mentoring process was the primary mode of experiential education linking a program participant with a highly competent and grass roots mentor and her/his community. Fourth, the design/duration embraced covenanting by participants to engage in active ministry among the poor and marginalized for one to two days a month over a nine month period (nine to eighteen days total) in about twenty-one sites with the total of twenty-eight participants (seven each from the four theological institutions in the Hyde Park Cluster).

This chapter is a tangible summary of some participants' theological reflections on the "Community Based Model" of the Chicago Local Immersion Project. The contributors are, Shirley Dudley (McCormick Theological Seminary [MTS] staff), Dow Edgerton (Chicago Theological Seminary [CTS] faculty), David Lindberg (Lutheran School of Theology in Chicago [LSTC] faculty), Janette Muller (LSTC Board member), Marilyn Olson (LSTC student), Joseph Pearce (MTS student), Roger Schroeder (CTU faculty), Mark Thompson (LSTC student), Harold Vogelaar (LSTC faculty), and Janice Wiechman (CTU student).

"THINK GLOBALLY AND ACT LOCALLY!"

Every participant was given the opportunity to reflect theologically on what has been popularly promulgated on an automobile bumper sticker, "Think Globally and Act Locally!" Through such reflections the participants were led to assess "optimal transformational educational experiences" in the diversified, multi-cultural contexts of the Metropolitan Chicago area.

The "Grass Roots" or "Base Community"

Throughout the Local Immersion Project, the participants were expected to carry out their assignments primarily by way of conversation with the members of local community-based educational programs with the guidance of the highly knowledgeable base community mentors. The set goals were to be with people in the context, to encourage them to develop their own agendas, and to become more conscious of the issues that are critical to them. Such goals were crucial for the immersion project and posed some challenges.

One of the facilitators of the reflection groups made the following initial observation at his first group meeting.

- *The first meeting focused on entry issues—first impressions and feelings, as one enters a "new world." However, the descriptions of one's site were quickly linked to initial questions of social structure, such as "Why is there prostitution, and who is really benefitting from this?" "Why are there homeless in this society?" "How can someone break the cycle of poverty in Cabrini Green [housing project]?"*

One participant remarked, "I was overwhelmed by the realization of how racism is embedded in our governmental systems and how bureaucracy works to keep it that way!" Another brought up a very interesting case study of the challenge of promoting and encouraging interfaith and cross-cultural interchange. In this particular case, he described his frustration in a particular church, where a Muslim was not allowed to enter the church and address the congregation. He found himself caught in a web of conflicting interests and values, between the parishoners, the pastor, and the parish committee.

The facilitator, then, interjected, "An important insight at this moment was that *globalization is local.*" At the same time, he remarked, "While this is a good case study, it demonstrates the tendency to jump too quickly to the question of 'What can I do in such a situation?'" While appreciating that everyone spoke and contributed to the discussion and sharing, the facilitator made a significant point in his observation, "Perhaps it would have been better if people would have focused more on their more personal issues as they immersed themselves, rather than jumping too quickly into theoretical questions." Nevertheless, he admitted that it was a good opening session, during which people already had begun seeing connections between their various present and past cross-cultural experiences and their current concerns.

As they continued their immersion programs, the participants thus realized the complexity of situations and the need to set realistic expectations for working within such situations. They were repeatedly reminded by the facilitator, however, of being stirred up and challenged by what they actually saw and experienced, rather than carrying out their own strictly theoretical discussion. His underlying warning concerned the avoidance of quick and simple solutions. "There is a need to let go of *my way* . . . to learn to find my appropriate place and role in such a situation," he commented, "for *it is important to listen and learn. . . .* It is a process of crossing over, step-by-step, and taking clues and invitations from the people. We need to start with their agenda, not ours, and we have to learn to 'go with the flow.'"

Two months later, at their third group meeting, the process proved to be well under way. It was described by the same facilitator as follows.

- *This was an excellent meeting, in which people identified and struggled with some personal and systemic issues arising within their sites. They were personally touched, confused, challenged, angered, and searching. People felt free to question, search, and learn from one another. They were involved and genuinely concerned with reflecting theologically on themselves as persons and ministers within situations of prejudice, abuse, injustice, and poverty: What is our response to evil?*

"Mission-in-Reverse"

The participants were led to assume the stance of a dialogical learning or a "bottom-up" methodology, in order to construct a relationship of mutuality and solidarity. Throughout such learning processes, they experienced ministries of "listening," or what has been termed as "mission-in-reverse" (*See* Chapter 5). The following story shared by one of the participants who worked at a westside congregation in Chicago alluded to the significance of that mode of Christian ministry.

- *At Christmas time I participated in a project called Angel Tree which linked several outlying evangelical churches to city families of prison inmates to provide Christmas gifts. The gifts were bought by the members of the outlying churches, wrapped and tagged on behalf of the incarcerated family member, and brought* to that church at the time of an event planned by its congregation on a Saturday afternoon in December. This event included the church people from all the churches, membership of that congregation, and the invited families of the prisoners.

The format for the afternoon was to provide refreshments and a short Sunday School lesson for the children and their parents in age groups, followed by a large gathering of all with entertainment, caroling, and the presentation of gifts—after the pastor preached and made an altar call.

The associate pastor had been working the crowd while the children were in their small-age-group meetings. He located several people, especially one man who had just been released from prison and had rejoined his family and had even found a job. They asked him for his testimonial about the changes in his life. He gave it willingly and this became one of the most moving moments of the afternoon. This gave more hope to the families gathered than any sermon ever could have.

Up to the point of the [pastor's] sermon, I felt the afternoon had a real cohesiveness and purpose that fit the context. There was excellent interchange among church folk, the event was well organized, people of all ages fulfilled their responsibilities with graciousness, and young people from all churches were heavily involved. Then it was time for the preacher to say, "Unless you have given your life to Christ, you will be damned." He said this in several ways in the next forty-five minutes, waiting for people to come down to the front of the church—in a way, the "carrot" for the altar call. There was a long silence. Finally two people came and were hustled away by members of the church. Everyone seemed to breathe a sigh of relief, because now it was time for this mountain of gifts that we had all been staring at to be distributed.

Something happened to me in this theological reflection, at least this way of expressing this firmly-held belief. Although the congregation and leadership were racially mixed, from different churches and social strata, people, in a short time, were beginning to make connections with each other no matter the differences. Yet now we were once again separated from one another on the basis of whether we were churched or unchurched, "saved" or "not saved," again whether we were the givers or the receivers of the gifts. I cannot fully put into words how this expression of theological conviction came across to me as a put-down for a group of people who were already feeling set apart and alienated.

"Bridge-building" as a ministerial formation

The participants' ministries were not only to do services for others but also to build up a trust relationship through service by embodying "reconciliation and unity" among the people in the community.

You read in Chapter 2 about one person who worked at the Genesis House (*See also* Chapter 7 by DePaul Genska). Dow Edgerton characterizes his experience as being "pressed upon the question of what it means for me to be a trustworthy person, and where the sources of trustworthiness are found." He continues, "The experience recalled for me some of my earlier roots in public ministry and parish ministry—settlement house work, mental health, etc. Teaching had distanced me from those experiences and the immersion re-connected me. I will continue to work at the Genesis House next year, in part because *I need to do so.*"

On this subject, one of the group reflection facilitators made this remark.

- *First of all, how do we understand the actual experience of people in a situation which is so different from our own? The case study for this issue was the experience of being with children and young people from Cabrini Green [housing project] at a large (mostly white and exclusive) Christmas affair in the Drake Hotel. Did the young African-American people experience this as exploitation, pleasure, injustice, enjoyment, racism, indifference, or frustration, poverty, etc?*

  After a rather lively discussion, it was clear that it is very difficult to try to understand someone else's experience. It is so easy to project one's own perspective. Furthermore, within the course of this discussion, there was an attempt to understand possible individual expectations of the African-American children within the social structure of Cabrini Green, with the situation of gangs, guns, drugs, and poor health care. Secondly, we dealt with the question of the relationship of the "outsider" minister and the community. What am I immersed into? Can we actually call it "immersion," since we can go home—we don't really live there? We have to deal with guilt and the further question of the what and why of evangelization. However there was also a strong sense that the immersion was important for helping us to be sensitized and knowledgeable about the other.

The person who worked at a shelter for the homeless in Uptown Chicago shared her experience as follows.

- *This opportunity has provided new insights in two areas in particular: the homeless now have faces and names and now I have questions about the terms on which we offer hospitality to the homeless.*

  Regarding the first, the experience has helped me to know the homeless more as human persons. They have names and faces. They come from a variety of situations. They are young, middle-aged, and old. They have good days and bad. On their good days, most wanted to relate with us in some way, they enjoyed a good laugh, and liked to tell of something that was important to them just like all human persons. I don't know much about their stories but rather know something of their "now." There are unique difficulties about their way of living—getting up early for day labor and not being sure if [you] will even be hired, carrying all [your] belongings each day, having minimal privacy. For some there seemed to be hope of getting off of the street; for others I was not so sure.

  The experience raises questions for me about the terms on which we offer hospitality to the homeless. . . . It seems that the hope and expectation is that these women are to be doing something to get back on their feet. Yet my own experience is that I am rather wiped out the day after spending the night at the shelter. Most of us go home and take a nap. I cannot live on that amount of sleep and function well. What, then, do the women feel? This is the amount of sleep they get—not one night a week, but every night. Now, I do not know why it is set up as it is, nor have I talked with the women about it. It did not seem my place to do so, but the experience has prompted me to do some thinking on the importance of discussing, with those being served, the effect of the service on them.

CRITICAL APPRAISAL OF THEOLOGICAL PRESUPPOSITIONS AND FRAMEWORKS

A participant who took part in both international and local immersion programs asserted, "The experience challenged my internal 'hierarchy' of gifts and skills." In particular reference to his experience at the Genesis House, he remarked,

> The House's interest in my cooking outweighed all the other abilities I brought. Or rather it became a safe and slow way for those abilities to be shared. When I was eventually asked to offer a religious service around the dinner table (a Passover Seder!), my place at the table made *sense*. I re-encountered connections among table celebration, hospitality, delight, and trust. The choice of international menus *always* turned the table talk to global topics, filtered usually through the experiences of local representations of those cultures.

The same participant provisionally summed up his reflections by stating, "The whole globalization experience (an Asian immersion plus the local immersion] has been of deep importance to me personally and professionally. My basic orientation toward theological education has been powerfully informed and transformed, particularly in relation to field-based learning. Our own institution's process of curricula has and will feel the impact of these experiences."

It is evident that the globalization of theological education is, with its multifaceted components, basically an interpersonal and transformative *process*. The process is intended to seek to augment "global awareness" and to enhance "self-discernment" by living and working in "global villages." Such processes occur by developing "cross-cultural competence," fostering a dynamic vision of the Christian community in ministry, and deepening "commitment to bear witness to the reconciling Gospel" among those who are being equipped for the ministries of the Church.

Globalization and contextualization are interdependent, in a similar way to the "local-global" interrelatedness and interaction (*See* Chapter 8). In fact, any thinking about context and locale often begins when the larger and global reality impinges, and vice versa; the two can serve as mutual correctives. The following articulation by a participant illustrates these dynamics.

- *Three issues are involved: 1) the overwhelming presence of poverty in North America and especially in other countries and the direct relationship of this poverty to the political and economic structures of our society. This is a spiritual and pedagogical problem; 2) globalization to me is another way to talk about under-*

represented constituencies, multiculturality, pluralism, and inclusivity. Attention to our local scene—Hyde Park as the center of one of the largest African-American communities in the U.S.—will require us to muster all of our resources in rethinking, rehearing, and serving; and 3) the challenge of other relations to Christians in every age.

Speaking of the challenge from the people of other religious communities, one participant (an Islamic scholar) included the following observation in his reflections:

▪ *More than ever, I feel there is a need for students to do at least some of their theological studies in dialogue with people of other faith commitments. If it is true that America has become a multicultural, multifaith society with no prospects of turning back, then it would be extremely shortsighted not to acknowledge this fact and to plan our ministerial training programs accordingly.*

We can, of course, continue as usual and let inertia carry the day, but why? With the presence of other faith communities right at hand, with Muslim, Buddhists, Hindus, Native Americans, and others as neighbors and colleagues, there is every reason to be in dialogue not just about what we believe, but why we believe what we do and the difference it makes. In the past we could learn about people of other faiths; now we can learn from them and with them. Nor is it enough just to live among each other; we must learn to live with each other, and even for each other, daring to believe that God is at work in and through the new culture being shaped.

In an attempt to define "globalization," one participant describes her experience as the "process by which we realize how interconnected we are. No longer can the events in the U.S.A. not have any impact on the rest of the world; the reverse is also true. Those inside of one country also impact each other in a much more significant way than was true in the past."

One participant in both international and local programs summarized as follows: "Because of my experience, I tend in conversation and dialogue to try and see things from the perspective of the 'other.' I have a limited ability to do this, of course, never being able to escape my own perspective, but the point of globalization seems to be that the possibilities are greater than one thinks, if one holds in mind the actual reality of the other—which is rooted in a specific socio-political-economic-religious identity."

Globalization and Crossing

Any "ministry" in the postmodern era, ever more fragmented, increasingly pluralistic, and rapidly changing, is *cross-cultural* by definition. It is a "crossing act, not merely socio-geographical and cultural but even theological, grounded upon the theology of incarnation or the *kenosis* of Christ (Phil. 2:7).

Every Christian has, therefore, an unprecedented challenge to bear witness to the Gospel across every conceivable boundary. Yet we observe that the anxiety of being able to stand at the cutting edge of our own "cultural" boundary is much greater than the anxiety of plunging into unfamiliar "cultural" contexts. One participant expressed her deep-seated anxiety in these words: "It has been a most challenging, enlightening, painful, frustrating, hopeful experience and I look forward to my involvement in the remainder of the year."

Another student participant recognizes such a crossing journey in his story:

■ *I am involved in a journey. I do not pretend to know where this will lead me. My experience of working with troubled youth in Florida has taught me the importance of not having to be in total control of the events going on around me. Without much acknowledgment from me, God was clearly at work in the efforts of those teenagers to help each other learn how to cope with some incredibly difficult situations. I was allowed to be part of that process. When asked why I was there (working twenty-four hours a day as the only counselor for ten twelve- to seventeen-year-old boys), I did not have a ready answer. When the day came that I was confronted with why someone should do something good or kind, rather than stab their neighbor, I was left standing with my tongue hanging out, muttering something about being a Christian. The young man promptly told me what I could do with my thoughts. What he suggested was anatomically impossible.*

  My reflection on that conversation, and similar ones, led me to enroll at the seminary in Hyde Park. I have undergone somewhat of a metamorphosis since arriving here in September of 1992. The workload has been challenging, but not nearly as challenging as the extracurricular activities in which I have been involved [such as the one] with the American Indian Center in Chicago as a part of my participation in the Local Immersion Project. As a result of this opportunity, I hope to continue to find the room to question, challenge, be challenged and grow in my awareness of how God interacts with different people.

How does one begin to explain the opening of souls between people? Only the Creator, through the spirit which unites us all, can make such things happen. My mentor and I have forged a bond which transcends the written and spoken word. What sticks with me is the awesome responsibility which underlies this union. I have been exposed to a new insight into the workings of the world. At least this insight is new for me, but ancient in the time of God. I have been asked to create a bridge. Isn't that ironic? The Creator leading me to create. The irony continues in that both ends of the bridge are grounded in the same Creator, the Great Spirit, God. . . . I am struck by the openness with which I have been received in light of these experiences. I have been ministered to. It is my responsibility and good fortune to share that ministry.

IMMEDIATE AND POTENTIAL IMPLICATIONS
FOR THEOLOGICAL EDUCATION

A certain amount of tension and even frustration was expressed among the participants, one of whom remarkably expresses this.

- *The reencounter over time provided a regular "shock" of changing context, experience, and issues. To move, in thirty minutes, from the setting of a faculty meeting into the kitchen of the Genesis House was a big jump—and the more at home I felt there, the bigger the jump seemed. Like your eyes becoming accustomed to the light, rather than turning on a flashlight, this change really helped tune my eyes and ears toward a more immediate sense of what is at stake in the language and saying of Christian faith.*

Toward the end of the nine-month journey, most of the discussions in reflection groups seemed to center around the area of making connections between globalization and seminaries. A basic question is, "Are we training pastors for maintenance, or for enabling (globalization in the world)?" "Do we need to revamp our academic program to allow space and energy for this goal of 'enabling'?" "What is a competent pastor?" One of the reflection group facilitators concluded,

> The group certainly felt that seminary training should include a process of integrating ministry and the real context of the world [globalization]. However, everyone in the group [both faculty and students] expressed their concern that they just don't have time and energy to take on globalization in addition to everything else. However, somehow, globalization issues have to be integrated within the overall system.

The group then proposed,

> Globalization in the seminaries can be approached at different levels: a) In terms of pedagogy, we encourage a teacher-student and student-teacher dynamic, which could allow more international and cross-cultural enrichment and exchange; b) globalization should affect the *curriculum, ethos,* and *governance* of the seminaries. Even the language used ("light" and "darkness") can reflect negative attitudes and prejudices towards other peoples.

A number of comments were made. First, in regard to *pedagogy:* "More references to world wide issues;" "Let international students participate even more in discussion and instruction;" "Real commitment to multicultural biblical criticism;" "Everything I do and all the experience I have affect my teaching because they affect who I am;" "I am more sensitive to ways in which social issues can become a part of our overall ministry rather than as 'outside agencies'"; "Get students and professors out of Hyde Park and into the neighborhoods and among the people of the city;" "We have so many required courses, but make it easier to be involved in the Hyde Park community—opportunities more publicized—practicum credit;" and, "Common accountability for globalization themes in all classes."

Second, in regard to *curriculum:* "I have tried recently to include more underrepresented constituencies in my bibliographies;" "Involve faculty/students from many cultures in overall planning;" "Better emphasis on offerings of cross-cultural courses;" "Have involvement both locally and globally as part of the curriculum or 'package' so that students can become involved without becoming overwhelmed;" "Initiate some team teaching with other seminaries, with the inclusion of local resources (people and agencies) in our curriculum;" "The incorporation of more cross-cultural experiences in the curriculum, along with exchanges with schools in other countries."

Third, in regard to *ethos:* "We need to be intentional about encouraging students to truly experience the city; I've known students who have not only spent their entire three academic years in Hyde Park but also all in LSTC. No wonder a friend of mine refers to this place as 'Hide Park';" "Putting more weight on the importance of communicating to other students, and eventually to a parish, how interrelated we are and that we can make a difference—partly by what we do in our own backyard."

"Become a seminary without walls!" seems to summarize all these comments.

While making these comments, one fundamental question arose, "What little can I do at the wider levels of the seminary and church structures?" "What is the strategic plan for this whole globalization project?" The participants were reminded of the importance of "balancing, listening, being, doing, and allowing."

These reflections lead us to conclude that the underlying theological thrust for the globalization of theological education is "contextual" or "local" in terms of basing on local communities, which was proven true through work in the community-based model employed for the Chicago Local Immersion Project. And contextual theologies are "indicative," "imperative," as well as "internal or incarnational" (*See* Stephen Bevans, *Models of Contextual Theology,* Orbis 1992), which the project participants stand ready to endorse.

10

Mentoring for Transformation

George F. Cairns

CONTEXTUAL STATEMENT

I am writing this reflection through the eyes of one of the mentors in the Local Immersion Project (LIP). As I mentioned in Chapter 5, I also served as the planning coordinator for the project. The reflections below will focus on my experiences as a developing mentor for students and others in a multicultural environment. I do not apologize for the confessional tone of this document nor do I present it as a particular example of excellence. It is simply the story of my work as minister/mentor and of my participation in this project.

There are as many stories of developing mentorships as there are mentors in this project. My particular story has the strength of embodying the particular mentoring philosophies of the Shalom Ministries Community (*See* Chapter 6) from the additional angle of one particular ministry as it develops over time, intersects with the project, and continues on after the project is completed. The nature of mentoring in the Shalom Ministries community is a lifelong commitment between members of the community and our grass roots mentors. While people and projects come and go, there is a deeply shared history that has developed between members of the Shalom Ministries community and several grassroots mentors.

I have come to understand that the mentoring process works at many levels between individuals and that it can also reach far beyond the one-to-one relationship that is the usually accepted model for mentoring. What best captures the sense of this process of relationship was once reflected by one Native American mentor to the Shalom Community when he said, "My heart shakes hands with your heart." This heart connection requires me to be as open to transformation as those who I apprentice.

I will explore both of these dimensions in the ministry of mentoring that has developed in my life over the past six years. I believe that authentic mentoring is always a two-way process of learning, so I will attempt to explore this dialogical process at these several levels. Where power relations exist (and where do they not), the mission-in-reverse theological principle of Shalom Ministries calls me to servant leadership. This means that I encourage the other person to take the lead, not by denying who I authentically am, with my skills and blind spots, but encouraging the other to develop our agenda. You see, we are in a dance, and I know that the powerless must have the lead.

BECOMING A MENTOR IN A MULTICULTURAL SETTING

The church where I am a member and where I work as minister of urban mission, the Peoples Church of Chicago, is a struggling inner-city church. Peoples Church is affiliated with two denominations, the United Church of Christ and the Unitarian Universalist Association. This church with a sanctuary which seats 1700 has gone from having white-gloved ushers, packed services, and national radio broadcasts of its services in the 1940s to, in 1994, having a congregation of about 150 who reflect the racial, economic, and cultural diversity of the current neighborhood. The church is heavily committed to a social justice ministry supporting community dinners, housing for a men's shelter, drop-in center for the homeless, and social service offices for a transitional housing program. The building houses a Korean UCC congregation and a Hispanic Episcopalian congregation as well as the ministries of Peoples Church.

The Urban Mission Program, a ministry of Peoples Church of Chicago, provides an institutional home for outreach and development within the Uptown section of Chicago.[1] Uptown is a neighborhood on the shore of Lake Michigan forty-eight blocks north of downtown Chicago. The writer and historian Studs Terkel calls Uptown "the United Nations of the have-nots."[2] On the lake front, people are living in $500,000 townhouses; within two blocks people are sleeping on the streets. It is an extremely diverse community—in the high school that serves this neighborhood, over sixty languages are spoken. There is a large Native American population. This neighborhood is a point of entry for new immigrants. One section, housing several ethnic groups from Southeast Asia, is called New Chinatown.

For the past twenty years, the adjoining neighborhoods of Edge-water and Uptown have been some of the primary places in the city where chronically mentally ill people have been "dumped" by an in-adequate mental health system. Mentally ill people continue to this day to be discharged from mental hospitals, even when hospital staff know that they have no place to live but a homeless shelter. Arguably, Uptown has more chronically mentally ill people than any other neighborhood in the country. There is also a Ku Klux Klan, Skinhead, and Nazi Party presence here.

There are other dynamics that pose additional challenges for minis-try in this context. There is the extreme fragmentation and alienation that arise from ethnic and cultural differences themselves. There is the isolation of new (and often times undocumented) immigrants. There is gang predation on other "street people."

There are systemic stressors too. Uptown has its own particular mix of special interest politics and economic pressures (particularly the cycle of real estate speculation) that provides an unusually challeng-ing environment for community reconciliation. There are also the city-wide systems that isolate communities and extract more resources from poor communities than they return. Then, too, there is the deteri-oration of all support systems that the Reagan/Bush administrations (with complicity from the rest of us) have engineered. The result is an extremely needy and fragmented community struggling to survive.

DEVELOPING A STREET MINISTRY

Peoples Church was also struggling for financial survival. Even so, during the spring of 1987, I was asked by the senior pastor of the church to examine how the church could better serve the larger com-munity. I talked with several grassroots people who knew the commu-nity well. We wanted to be of service, but not to compete with already existing services. From these conversations it became clear that, given my background as a clinical psychologist, a street ministry with homeless people would fulfill an unmet need.

I was a "second career" student at Chicago Theological Seminary studying for my Master of Divinity degree. My plans were to become a spiritual director, to add one more credential to my list, and to continue on, pretty much as before, as a clinical psychologist who would do psychotherapy with new skills to better help people explore deeper issues of meaning in their lives. Beginning a street ministry was the furthest thing from my mind. This path not only did not fit with my career aspirations, but it was also distasteful to me for two other reasons.

First, I felt pulled backward by my past as a psychologist. I had worked for many years with poor people, many of whom were chronically mentally ill, in very difficult settings in the inner city, and also in an isolated rural area. I knew how personally demanding this work was. One reason I had entered seminary was to switch gears in order to revitalize my work. Working as a street minister seemed suspiciously like the work that I had been doing for the past fifteen years.

Second, many of the potentially novel aspects of street ministry also had negative connotations for me. I had left the church because of my feeling that the church addressed neither the spiritual nor the physical needs of the people I was serving. In addition, I was repulsed by the heavy-handed evangelism and repressive views of family that were foisted on the poor by some of those church groups. Who better represents the worst of these stereotypes than the street-corner evangelist, handing out tracts and demanding mechanically that others accept this prepackaged religion? My worst fears were realized some time later when one of my professors at the seminary remarked on the "wonderful work of evangelism" I was doing. Only later did I begin to understand how the "detoxified" evangelism that he saw taking place in this ministry reflected not my worst fears, but a deeper and more authentic way of being in service with others.

Even with these substantial reservations, I was drawn to begin this ministry. During my first full day on the streets, I noticed a large number of police cars and ambulances blocking the street two blocks from the church. Someone had been killed, although no one knew the details. Later I found out that a Catholic sister, a friend of the poor, had been killed by a mentally ill man she had taken in.

One of my first teachers, a street minister who worked with teenagers after midnight, showed me the neighborhood and pointed out places where many drug deals come down or where people had been killed, and which bars one could enter only with great care. He showed me "murder alley," a dogleg alley where the recesses cannot be seen from the two major streets it connects. He taught me about the uneasy relationship we have with the police. The beat cops either ignored us or, sometimes, hassled us. While this had the disadvantage of feeling like, at best, an unstable truce, it decreased the chances of my being viewed as a "snitch."

Even so, I heard from some of my street friends that the word was out that I was a "narc" who was working undercover. On the streets, everyone has an agenda. Over the first few months of being on the street, when I didn't come across like the stereotypes of the street minister that others had for me (and which I feared becoming), people assumed a hidden and more sinister agenda. A "rep" as a "narc" is not a good one to have—it can get you hurt.

You should know that I am a rather large and hairy fellow. I have noticed when I'm not wearing a clerical collar, sometimes at night people will cross the street to keep some distance from me. So, not suprisingly, after a period of months, one guy asked me if I was an ex-biker. I told him that I had ridden bikes when I was younger, so he labeled me "Father George, the biker priest." From then on, people seemed to have "made" me and accepted me for who I am.

As I walked the streets, wearing a clerical collar, I understood that people were projecting onto me their feelings about the church. In psychological language, I was a walking "Rorschach inkblot test." Many of the poor are not happy with the way they have been treated by the church and expressed their anger as they talked with me. They found out that I was angry about many of the same issues. Then it was possible to reenter scripture and prayer in a different way and discover a deeper story that fit who we are. Slowly, the street people and I "detoxified" the scriptures so that much of the language we both had found so oppressive lived in a new way in us. We mentored each other. Deep learnings took place. Strongly-held convictions and past brokennesses were healed.

Staying with people to go beyond our superficial initial encounters is a spiritual practice for me. I have heard every "con" that I believe the human mind can create—and the variations, too! Staying with the person sometimes moves us to a deeper place.

One day I was walking down the street with a friend when a man stopped and asked me for five dollars for the bus. He must have thought that I just fell off the potato truck. I asked him "Where are you headed—Peoria?" He laughed and continued telling me how he had lost his business, was now broke and homeless. By this time I could smell alcohol on his breath. When he finally hit me with his bottom-line request for one dollar, I again refused. He then brought out the big guns and said, "If Jesus was here he would give me a dollar." I replied, "If Jesus were here he wouldn't give you a dollar because he would smell alcohol on your breath and believe that you would use this money to harm yourself. What I will do is to walk with you to the detox center near here, and once you're straight, help get you on your way." We talked for a while longer. He refused my offer. I gave him my card and asked him to give me a call any time. As he walked, he turned back to face me and said, "You know if Jesus were here he wouldn't give me a dollar today." We never saw each another again.

DEVELOPING BASE CHRISTIAN COMMUNITIES

As I became better known on the street, one of the social workers who worked with women asked me if I "would do Bible study" in one of the transient hotels (SROs). I agreed to hang out in a room at the hotel and announce my availability. If people asked me to do Bible study, I would do so. After about a month of talking with people, two women asked me if I would begin a Bible study group. I agreed, and we have continued this as part of our community meetings the residents call "The Northmere International Friendship Club" after their residence and owing to the fact that our membership is multicultural and multiracial.

This mode of ministry with the poor has stretched both Peoples Church and our denomination. When I became a licensed minister, I was allowed to offer communion in only one church. When I explained to our church and ministry committee of the denomination that my church was the Uptown neighborhood of Chicago, we were all challenged to rethink our definition of church and congregation. They kindly allowed Uptown to be my church for purposes of licensure.

A friend gave me a beautiful gold chalice and paten that their community was not using. My first thought was that it was just too fancy, that it would be too great a contrast with our meeting rooms with falling plaster and roaches running from us when we first come in. Instead of making the decision myself, I asked our worship groups. They said that because this communion set was so different, it would make communion seem that much more powerful for them. My grassroots mentors help me appreciate the way liturgy speaks to them. The liturgy speaks to me in new ways, too.

When I first came to the hotel, the people who sought my advice were passive, mostly speaking only when spoken to and offering few ideas or comments themselves. As we got to know each other, people began making suggestions; they suggested forming the friendship club out of the Bible study group and began to plan for recreational events that could involve other people at the hotel.[3] The club ordered T-shirts for the whole hotel and jackets for the board members of the club. They prepared gifts of toiletries for new residents, who usually had little, coming as they did from the shelters, hospitals, and jails.

None of the residents who first came to Bible study still live in the hotel. Some have been killed; others have died of "natural causes;"[4] still others are in nursing homes, mental hospitals, in jail or have disappeared back to the streets. I am profoundly struck by how little continuity there is in this community. Members of the club are doing things to develop our collective memory. There are now more regularly visiting members of the club who have moved out and live nearby. Club members have also developed a newspaper that provides news not only for all residents of the hotel, but also for those who have moved on.

People are finding their voices through this newspaper. They are now writing stories and poems, contributing artwork, and even producing the paper in the hotel. Many are serving others in the hotel. Several have joined the congregation at Peoples Church. Several help others to church on Sunday and volunteer at the community dinners. Their presence in the activities of the Peoples Church has moved us to a new level of worship, pastoral care, and scripture study.

MENTORING THE LOCAL CHURCH TO BECOME A PLACE OF HOSPITALITY

Initially I was asked to mediate between longtime members of the congregation and the homeless people who had begun to join us for worship. One Christmas, I noticed a woman sitting in the shadows in the back of the sanctuary. She wore many layers of clothes, topped with a red blanket that shrouded her face. It was as if some grim Christmas spirit were among us. During the first few months that I knew her, she spoke only to answer "yes" or "no" to direct questions, except one week when a beat cop drove her from her favorite spot on a bus bench. She rewarded him with a rich nonstop stream of invective that was at least a minute in length. Some members of the congregation were afraid of or hostile toward people like her, but as we joined in Bible study, where people heard one another's stories, we went beyond the surface markers of class and race. People who had said to me that all the people in the shelter were bums, as they got to know the men who live among us, moved beyond these safe stereotypes and have begun to experience the pain and joy of persons whose lives are so different, and who live often unnoticed among us.

Soon, others joined with us in the Urban Mission Program. One of the first students was a cook. He began what has become our community dinner program where about 140 people come together for a sit-down meal served both by local people and people from partner churches. Here, too, we began with a more shallow notion of being in service than we realized. Our agendas were driven primarily by our own needs and talents. We had a skilled cook, a hungry community, and a sense that we wanted to be hospitable to others, so we dispensed with the "soup kitchen" language and relabeled what we were doing "dinners with the community." We knew enough to encourage people who were helping to serve the dinners (mostly people from suburban churches) to eat with the people from the community. Even so, we began by providing service, and the people from the community acting as the passive recipients, much like the old soup kitchens. Over the next few years, we encouraged everyone to pitch in and help. Now, it is very difficult to distinguish the "helpers" from "those being helped" as we work together offering one another our skills. Here, too, people who have viewed themselves as victims, as passive consumers of services, have become engaged participants in their (and our) lives.

MENTORING THE LARGER CHURCH

Over the past six years, literally hundreds of people have come to visit with us and exchange ideas about multicultural ministry. In visits of lengths from a few hours to several days, we have exchanged ideas and methods with people in urban ministry from all over the world.

There are dangers here. This is spiritually dangerous work. There is much pain and despair. Telling our story helps to alleviate our shared pain, but it also can be an opportunity for us both to exploit the suffering of those we are in service with and to become self-righteous as we tell our story. I don't have any easy answers here. I feel that, to the extent that we share our common work, acknowledging the differences in class and economic privilege, our struggles with living in these different worlds, and our continuing commitment to the process, we can mitigate these dangers. I know my friends among the poor are kind to me. They tell me I work too hard and they celebrate with me when I have a chance to leave the city. I don't know how I can adequately return these kindnesses.

My struggle is mirrored as we engage with people from privileged churches who primarily assist us in our community dinners. Part of the covenant that we have with our friends in the partner churches is that we have briefing and debriefing sessions on a regular basis. At first, our work is to encourage one another to move beyond stereotypes. One rather wealthy person said one evening following a dinner, "I'm surprised, I thought that the people at the dinners would be much skinnier—some people even seem overweight." At times like this I monitor my internal rage, and attempt to realize the callous ways in which I live my life, being in two such different worlds. The gift that this can bring is to continue to open my eyes to the realities of these two worlds, and to encourage others to do so, too. So my response to this person (rather than anger) was to talk about how poor nutrition coming only from cheap foods often makes one overweight, so she and I could move to another level of engagement.

The role-blending at the dinners is not always easy for ourselves or our partner church friends. It is much easier to have the dinners preprogrammed, with defined jobs and preplanned schedules. The reality we face, in a place where pipes often break, where drains almost always clog, where stoves stop working, and where there are fights and medical emergencies, is that we are led to open ourselves to the unexpected and to trust that God will not mock our work together. Too often we criticize ourselves and accept criticism from our suburban friends for " . . . not being organized enough." You see, we are sharing in the life of our community, doing the best we can, and ministering on the edge as do those we serve. We have left behind the safe harbors of premanaged solutions, are sharing in the reality of this community, and encourage others to join with us. Students from the seminaries often take this invitation.

MENTORING DURING THE GLOBALIZATION PROJECT

During the LIP, one student, Terry Bozich, worked as a minister of urban mission as part of her field placement from Chicago Theological

Seminary. Her primary work was in two of the transient hotels and in the community dinners. She is a gifted teacher and learner. She was quickly accepted by the groups at the hotels. Her openness played a significant part in this acceptance. Another reason for it is the repeated experience that I have had with a transfer of trust that grows out of long-term relationships in a community. Since people know that others from our church and I have been with them for several years, an outsider who is a friend of ours may quickly become a friend of theirs.

There is also the movement of the ongoing process that provides cohesion for our relationships together. The rhythm of our meeting times, outings together, the shared prayer and extension of our stories together provide an entry for the outsider to quickly become an insider. There are still tests that the newcomer must pass. "How long will you stay?" "Are you a 'real' minister?" "Can I borrow five bucks until Monday?"

There continue to be tests for me. "Are these students who are working trustworthy?" When we have visitors, "Who are they and why have they come here?" I feel obligated to introduce outsiders only when they are ready to be with the community in respectful and kindly ways. Otherwise I violate the trust my grassroots mentors have given me.

This gatekeeping involves a dance. When are changes—proposed by a newcomer, but resisted by me—disrespectful, and when are they only counter to my own lack of vision and inertia? Ultimately, this is a question that can only be answered by the community—by our grassroots mentors. These are direct people; they tell us when we have missed the point. Each Easter, I bring hot cross buns to our Bible study. One Easter after I had brought some buns from a wonderful (and expensive) Swedish bakery, one member of the club asked, "Where'd you get these, the ones at the [local supermarket] are much better." They also vote with their feet. If we have not adequately involved people in the planning from the beginning, and have an ill-timed or unpopular program, it simply isn't well-attended. In this community, there are few pretensions and little tolerance for doing something dumb. Life is too short and too precarious, with little insulation of wealth to smooth the rough spots.

Terry brings particular skills in art and music. She quickly identified one member of our group, Carl, who is a wonderful keyboard player and composer. He gifted the group with his playing and with tapes of his new compositions. Simultaneously the group, Carl, she, and I are enriched by this process of Terry identifying her skills, and encouraging our friend Carl to mentor himself and us.

My presence as a model of servant leadership is to be led by my grassroots mentors and by Terry. Encouraging her over time to take the lead in conversation and planning with the group resulted in her more frequently standing in my place. She, along with members of the club, is coming to the church more and more regularly—coming in a group and wheeling one club member in a wheelchair. In turn, these wonderful people have transformed our Sunday worship, encouraging an interactive style of conversational sermons, "interrupting" the service as the spirit moves them, and opening each of us to new ways of understanding the deep meaning of hospitality—a process of giving gifts to one another, recognizing the power of each of these gifts, and passing them along.

The occasions when Terry and I reflected, away from our grassroots teachers, offered us times of prayer, joyful lunches, and personal reflections on the joys and struggles crossing these boundaries are bringing to us. Issues of systemic evil are seen, but now through the experiences of those whom we are with. Evil moves from the abstract and ideological, into the concrete lived experience of our teachers—and to the extent that we "get it," to ourselves. In response we are compelled to respond in concrete ways, to experience small "zones of liberation,"[5] glimpses of God's realm, as we struggle together to reduce oppression in people's lives—one by one and now in small base community after small base community. Here too we try to be led by our grassroots mentors. They are developing the agendas to engage the powers and principalities;[6] we offer ourselves as agents of these agendas, bringing our own unique skills, but we encourage them to lead us.

This past year people from the hotels organized, drew up, and circulated a petition advocating better mental health care coverage in the upcoming comprehensive federal health care plan. Recently in church, one of the organizers proudly read a reply from one of our United States senators.

CONTINUING THE PROCESS IN THE COMMUNITY

The work of the Urban Mission Program continues. Pastor Bozich continues to work in two hotels and assists with the community dinners as a staff member of the church. Two additional students from

Chicago Theological Seminary are in field placements at Peoples Church this year. Others have joined the staff and the congregation, so new programs such as employment training and transitional housing projects are developing as a result of these efforts. All of the base Christian communities continue and new communities are being formed.

Through the leadership of Terry and others, more and more of our community dinners are being served by people from the community itself. People who, four years ago, came, sat, ate, and left, are now planning menus, preparing, serving, and cleaning the community dinner space. These same people are more actively involved in the long-term planning of these dinners. Clear shifts are happening within our congregation, where people from the transient hotels are taking increasing leadership, developing the vision of the entire church.

I believe that mentoring for servant leadership always prepares for the elder to erode the need for his or her presence from the very beginning of apprenticeship. This is true for programs as much as it is for individual apprenticeships. The day before I wrote this, I formally announced at the annual meeting of Peoples Church that I will leave the church as a minister of urban mission within the next six months. New leadership has developed at the grassroots level and among the clergy who have joined us on this journey. I believe it is time for me to fade from this program, to realize that the collective vision that has developed over the years must be sustained by others if it is to grow. This transition challenges me to learn how to move on, to serve the people in Uptown by my absence, those in a new community, perhaps, by my presence, and to more deeply acknowledge that God's mysterious movement in the world mentors all of us as we continue.

REFLECTIONS ON THE PROCESS

The most consistant and deepening experience that I continue to have is that no one, particularly myself, can attempt to stand outside the process of transformation without dramatically reducing the effectiveness of the mentoring relationship. By being open to the unexpected, the gift of the other, especially the gift of the enemy,[7] we both offer ourselves for transformation and present an opportunity for the other also to be transformed. It is no accident that Gandhi subtitled his autobiography, "A history of my experiments with truth."[8] This book describes the life of a powerful mentor who dramatically changed systems, and who also intentionally practiced a spirituality of opening to the other in creative ways.

The challenges to live this kind of life are great. By extending ourselves to transformation, we change, often in fundamental ways. How do we maintain a sense of personal integrity in the midst of these shifts? For me, this search requires a deep faith in the creative opportunity that God offers me, and a community of support and accountability which provides a reality check on these movements of the heart and mind.

In a community of mentors, such as Shalom Ministries, I can better identify my gifts and blind spots, become more open to these limitations, and respond creatively to the challenges that they offer. I can also seek the assistance of others whose gifts complement mine so that we can systemically multiply the aggregation of our gifts.

There is deep work to be done here. Mentoring is not simply the transformation of individuals' ideas about the other. It involves systemic shifts in our full-bodied[9] understanding of what it is to be a human being. In our tradition, the normative mentor for becoming fully human is Jesus of Nazareth.

Jesus as Mentor. In his fascinating examination of Jesus as mentor, Aaron Milavec examines this process of deep transformation of individuals and systems.[10] Using hints from scripture and other contemporaneous sources, he examines ways in which Jesus mentored for transformation. He uses Polanyi's notions of implicit knowing to explain how, through apprenticeship, deep understandings can be transmitted between master and apprentice.[11] He elegantly describes the process of deepening understanding of the seemingly paradoxical inaccessibility/accessibility of a chess rule because

> Only at the end of an appropriate apprenticeship, when the novice has tacit skills which rival those of the master, does the rule become transparent to the depth of meaning that the master intends.[12]

Further light is shed on this process of acquiring deep full-bodied insights by the philosopher Gregory Bateson,[13] who applied Bertrand Russell's theory of logical types to the concept of learning. His intent, as is mine, is " . . . that the barriers which divide the various species of behavioral scientists (including transformative educators) can be illuminated . . ."[14] by such notions. This theory states that

No class can, in formal or logical discourse, be a member of itself; that a class of classes cannot be one of the classes which are its members; that a thing is not the thing named. . . . Somewhat less obvious is the further assertion of the theory: that a class cannot be one of those items which are correctly classified as non-members. . . . Lastly, the theory asserts that if these simple rules of formal discourse are contravened, paradox will be generated and the discourse vitiated.[15]

Russell's theory proposes a hierarchy of more and more abstract classes, with less-abstract classes nested within higher-order classes. For example, the class "chair" is of one level of logical type; the class "non-chair" is of the same level. They are both nested within the logical class "furniture" which is a class of the classes "chair" and "non-chair." If one formally attempts to treat the logical class "furniture" the same as its class members "chair" or "non-chair," logical problems arise.

Bateson applied this notion to describe a set of classes of learning labeled Learning I through Learning III. Each higher class contains within it the lower classes of learning.[16] Let me explain.

Learning I. This is what lay people usually mean by learning. "These are cases where an entity gives at time two a different response from what it gave at time one. . . . "[17] This covers a broad range of learning, from a rat learning which turn to make in a maze to a person learning to play a Bach fugue. With repeated practice, new responses occur. These kinds of learning are often called trial-and-error learning, instrumental learning, or conditioning. In the globalization project, examples of this level of learning are acquiring new data so they can be discussed regarding places, people and institutions and learning schedules of work.

Learning II. This next higher type is learning about learning. "Various terms have been proposed in the literature for various phenomena of this order; 'deutero-learning', 'set learning', 'learning to learn' and 'transfer of learning' may be mentioned."[18] This is learning about the context in which learning takes place. For example, when I first learn to play a piece on the piano, it may take me a long time to play it with few errors. As I continue to play new pieces, the time for learning to the same level of performance will decrease. I have learned to recognize a class of behaviors, "piano playing," and to transfer learned skills from one member of that class, "Bach fugue," to another, "Chopin étude."

As described in more detail below, much of this kind of learning takes place out of awareness. Learned patterns may become more and more generalized, and may ultimately color a person's global expectations. The person may then anticipate that the world is mostly punishing or mostly rewarding, structured or unstructured. Bateson argues that these more general relational patterns develop early and also quickly drop outside of awareness.[19] He suggests that what is learned is a ". . . way of *punctuating events.*"[20] What then happens is that we often mold our world to ". . . fit the expected punctuation."[21] This self-validating process is very difficult to erode because it is out of awareness and the person unconsciously manipulates the environment in a way that assures other learning opportunities are missed.

This process can be so general that primary attributes of an individual's personhood result. "In describing individual human beings, both the scientist and the layman commonly resort to adjectives descriptive of 'character'"[22] to denote the results of Learning II.

Examples of Learning II abound in our cultural presuppositions. It is only when we encounter these presuppositions, when we name and challenge them, that their habitual character may be eroded. Examples of Learning II are to equate poverty with "thinness" as the affluent woman mentioned above did, to equate poverty with helplessness, and to equate wealth and education with wisdom.

I argue that it is precisely the process of freeing ourselves from these kinds of unconscious patterns that constitutes transformative education. The learning processes that facilitate this freedom are what Bateson calls Learning III. I extend an examination of these processes to include Learning IV.

Learning III. This level involves the ability to expand the set of alternatives, or, as Bateson states, "Learning III is change in the process of Learning II, e.g., a corrective change in the system of sets of alternatives from which choice is made."[23] It may be described as a powerful shift in perspective or as a breakthrough in understanding. Previously constricted awareness is now unbound, and new ways of understanding are available. But

> Learning III is likely to be difficult and rare even in human beings. Expectably, it will also be difficult for scientists, who are only human, to imagine or describe this process. But it is claimed that something of this sort does from time to time occur in psychotherapy, religious conversion, and in other sequences in which there is profound reorganization of character.[24]

One example of Learning III took place in the mentoring project when one participant attempted to get information by phone regarding an African-American grassroots movement within the city's fire union. He was looking specifically for a copy of the newsletter that this group was circulating. After making many phone calls to city and union officials, being stonewalled and transferred, he was at a loss about how to proceed. One day, while talking with an African-American colleague about these difficulties, the colleague suggested that he go to the firehouse close to the seminary and ask one of the African-American firefighters for a copy. Our colleague did so and was given a copy of this paper. He reflected on this shift in awareness in our reflection meetings. Here, a shift in his understanding of the context took place. The usual responses to seeking information (phone calls, follow-up to persons in authority) failed and a new strategy (talking directly with a grassroots individual, rather than an official) developed. Here, too, the participant articulated his awareness of the limitation of the previous habitual pattern and how the expanded vision was helpful.

Learning IV.[25] I would extend our examination to Learning IV, a higher order class of learning which would have as its primary characteristic the ability to move among all of the lower levels of learning and, in particular, which would make readily available the multiple shifts in perspective of the sorts described in Learning III.

If speaking about Learning III is fraught with difficulty, attempting to describe Learning IV is even more perilous. The very definition of Learning IV, developing the ability to cross boundaries of different learning types, suggests that paradoxes and other logical difficulties may, by definition, arise from attempting to capture this phenomenon in logical discourse. Put another way, my extension of the Bateson theory implies that much of the "ineffability" of such "mystical experience" may not lie in the phenomenology of the experience itself. Rather, the difficulty of expressing "Learning IV experiences" in logical discourse reflects an epistemological limitation of what it is to be human.

I propose that transformational education encourages Learnings III and IV to occur. That is, transformational learning involves becoming more open to seeing the world from multiple viewpoints and to shifting among these perspectives with increasing skill. This kind of learning has the seemingly paradoxical characteristics of highly focal attention combined with intentional rapid shifts of perspective. The dynamics underlying Learning III and IV are poorly understood by mainstream Western psychology and education. There are hints regarding these dynamics in the contemplative literature from both the East and West.

In Christian tradition, Christ provides the perfect example of a person who demonstrated this quality of compassionate presence in all aspects of his life. His life provides us with a model of someone who demonstrates Learning III and IV. Along with Milavec and others, I believe that Christ is also the normative transformative educator.[26]

Many Christians seek to live their lives "in the imitation of Christ" and saints, past and present. We often fall short of our intentions. Deep dynamic spiritual and psychological processes underlie these ways of living, which are ultimately ways of being.

Merton argues that it is critically important in all cross-cultural dialogue to better understand ourselves and our presuppositions.[27] This uncovering is unlikely to occur without intentional effort to stimulate deepening dialogue. A variety of methods can be of assistance here. One that is explored elsewhere in this volume, which has deeply influenced my work, has developed within the Shalom Ministries community. There are many others. Suffice it to say that I urge us to continue to explore these methods intentionally and intensively.

With Jesus as model, mentoring is ultimately a subversive process for people and systems to become more fully human. Milavec notes that

> Without the reincorporation of apprenticeships under competent masters within the churches, any saintly wisdom will be isolated in a few graced individuals and systematically ignored by the masses who are quite pleased with their Sunday Christianity and their privatized religious experiences.[28]

I would add that we need such mentors if globalization in theological education is not to suffer a similar fate.

11

Individual and Social Transformation

George F. Cairns

INTRODUCTION: AN ANTHROPOLOGY OF SYSTEMS

As this project developed, it became clear to us that the anthropology that was developing to describe us as individuals may also apply to the larger systems in which we are embedded. We have come to understand that the possibilities for individual human change and transformation are mirrored in our institutions. In reflection, we as individuals are complicit with the action and inaction inherent in these larger systems.

Recently, the New Testament scholar Walter Wink theologically examined such systemic embeddedness in a series of works, the most recent of which is *Engaging the Powers*.[1] Using the first-century notions of the early church, Wink argues that good and evil exist in systems that often seem almost to take on a life of their own. These powers and principalities are expressed today in terms like "corporate culture," "mission statements," and cultural presuppositions.

He has specifically examined the spirit of these institutions and their fall and possibilities for redemption. He argues that individual and systemic redemption are inextricably joined. The processes that apply to systemic transformation are mirrored in individual transformation, and vice versa.

Another helpful body of work that resonates with Wink's systemic and organic world is that of the anthropologist and philosopher Gregory Bateson. While Wink examines the spirit within individuals and systems, Bateson examines how systems know. He has described systemic processes from the smallest sentient beings to world systems as minds that have the same patterns connecting stability and change as do individual organisms. Bateson has examined the relatedness of

153

communication within and among such systems as a way to describe their fundamental ways of knowing.

Bateson argues that mind is a relational process rather than a thing (a disengaged process) contained within another thing (the brain/body). While highly abstract, his criteria for mind have profound implications for an engaged knowing.[2] Central to his view is the understanding that mind is not limited to the process contained within a single individual human organism.[3]

This stance requires that we regard "mind" as an interpenetrating process that includes different people and other actors at different times. Thus this stance requires us to question our usual notion that our mind is only that process residing within the boundary of our physical body and is somehow radically separate from others. This understanding is amazingly similar to that of William Ernest Hocking, the great Protestant mystic, theologian, and philosopher, who stated that he was convinced "'with the force of an intuition' that 'the supposed isolation of (individual) minds is an illusion.'"[4] This contemplative perspective, grounded in experience and deeply appreciative of our multiple relationships, offers us concrete strategies for transformation.

What is implied is that, to the extent that patterns of relationship we call mind and spirit do connect individuals with one another and with systems, similar methods for change may bring about the transformation of both. Both Wink and Bateson examine the patterns that connect, and propose that change (and redemption in Wink's analysis) of both individuals and the systems they inhabit are inextricably linked. They suggest a deeply incarnational and organic worldview by which individual and social systems share their ways of being.

The two most critical institutions for us in theological education are the church and the seminary. Both are mature systems with long standing histories and traditions. Both have been characterized in organic, systemic ways. Scripture describes the church as the Body of Christ (I Cor. 12)—theological intuitions that are congruent with this contemporary incarnational and organic worldview. Leonardo Boff has cited this scripture passage and other sources within scripture and tradition to argue for a more organic ecclesiology, based on function and service rather than on power.[5] It is in this sense that the organic metaphor is used here.

The seminary is also characterized in organic terms. It derives from the root *seminarium*, a seed plot, and is used to describe places of growth and nurture for plants, humans, and non-human animals. It encompasses notions of physical, educational, and spiritual nurture.[6] Too often we as educators only notice the nurture of the seed plot on the developing seeds. We fail to appreciate the organic interdependence and profound effect that the developing life has on the seed bed. Gregory Bateson elegantly described the coevolution of the *Eohippus* and the grassy plains that it inhabited.[7] The horse not only adapted to living on the plain, but the plain changed because of the horse's presence. Bateson argues what evolved (or coevolved) was not the horse or the plain, but the context.

I believe that this project has suggested ways in which change may be effected in both of these institutions using an organic anthropology of systems that is implicit throughout this project—an anthropology of interdependent (and interpenetrating) individual and social transformation.

MENTORING THE TRANSFORMATION OF SYSTEMS

I am just beginning to examine how this anthropology might be applied for change in our institutions. Our experiences leading up to the Local Immersion Project and the project itself do suggest some helpful strategies. I have seen some institutional changes that have grown out of our collective experience. In Chapter 9 Yoshiro Ishida described some of these changes that grew out of our theological reflections, while in Chapter 10 I detailed the process of mentoring larger systems in one community context. What I would like to do below is suggest some ways to extend some of these current understandings to other contexts.

Mentoring Systems. Our fundamental understanding is that we who are engaged in this fluid relationship of mentoring individuals *can* act as effective mentors for our institutions as well. Our planning model, described in Chapter 5, of a ritual journey into the wider world in order to seek new understandings for the home community has been borne out by our experience. As described by several authors in this volume, participants have acted as carriers of important new understandings back to their home seminaries. I have described in Chapter 10 some ways that the congregation and the larger church were mentored from the grassroots experiences of our one-to-one mentoring process. Are there some ways in which this process may be generalized? The theological principles practiced by the Shalom Ministries Community which were critical in developing many aspects of this project provide one set of lenses through which to see possibilities for more general systemic change. These four theological principles, detailed in Chapter 5, provide us with a praxis-based approach to examine individual and systemic change.

Mission-in-Reverse. Fully listening to the other, mission-in-reverse, as the people in Shalom Ministries use the term, provides us an opportunity for radical openness to the other. What this means institutionally is that we must listen carefully to the voices of one another and encourage respectful change for ourselves and the institution. Our fates are so inextricably linked. It is particularly important where power relations exist institutionally that we more carefully listen to those who are in a powerless position. Throughout the project we endeavored to be led by those who are more marginalized in our "bottom-up" planning process. Mission-in-reverse calls us to a different rhythm of engagement, where we listen, wait and listen again to the marginalized. We are continually challenged to take risks—to open ourselves to others' agendas. For institutions, this stance increases the permeability of the institution to the larger community. It suggests that we develop institutional ways to increase the impact the larger world has on the institution. This project has been one such institutional praxis.

Developing Base Christian Communities. Our friends in the two-thirds world have offered us a powerful organizational model. In particular, we understand that the poor and marginalized have the lead in our relationships. If we are to erode existing power relations, this must be so. Institutionally, this implies that we must join with the poor and the marginalized both within and outside our institutions. If we are to be Christian and church, we must include prayer, worship, theological reflection, and mission in our community life. If this is to be true community, *koinonia,* it is an engagement that reflects the intensity and commitment present in many of the one-to-one mentoring relationships described in this project. This suggests that our churches and institutions must become more intentional about each of the dimensions of what it means to be at the Base and Christian and in community.

Contextualization. We must, if we are to be respectful, carefully assess our institutional openness and rigidities just as we do our own and the openness of our communities. If we are to change together successfully, we must understand our differences and respect them. How can we sensitively assess where we are as individuals and institutions?

Models of adult learning describe maps for the developmental territory of mature individuals and may provide help understanding institutions.[8] It also is important that we draw new maps. Laurent Daloz has demonstrated how such developmental maps can be used to facilitate individual transformation for individuals in the mentoring process.[9] I suggest that such maps may also be used to determine the developmental status of institutions such that we can more sensitively match our pedagogy with the readiness of the institution or the subgroup within the institution which we engage.

Developmentalists realize that not all aspects of functioning within the individual neatly follow the trend of development. Some "fluid positioning" may be taking place in some areas of a person's cognitive life while others may be functioning in relativistic or dualistic ways.[10] Is this not also reflected systemically where certain individuals and groups within an institution have more open and contextual worldviews than others?

Note the paradox that such a developmental approach poses to Bateson's notions of levels of learning described in Chapter 10. We have two dramatically different perspectives: that fluid changes in perspective are *always* available epistemologically to both individual human beings and larger systems—in Bateson's notions of learning classes; and that in practice, their application unfolds over a period of time measured developmentally in minutes to decades. Here we see one of the central paradoxes of transformation made explicit—that transformation is always available to us, and its realization often takes disciplined praxis over extended periods of time for it to happen.

Whether the breakthroughs to transformation happen suddenly or over extended time periods, I believe that the learning system exhibits certain relational characteristics. I would define the fully mature learning system as multifocal, able to understand its context, able to act in this context, and able, simultaneously, to reflect on the implications of this praxis for the next action. It is critical that we realize that the map is not the territory—that our engaged praxis is the territory and that the maps emerge *from* our collective praxis—and that we therefore do not stand outside the maps but are the co-creators of them with all of the attendant limitations and creativity that come with such an endeavor.

Bridge-Building. We understand that boundary-crossing is crucial for this process of openness to be maintained. Bridge-building by individuals and institutions can provide the stickiness to hold us together through the rough spots. We realize that there is much embedded power and inertia in things staying as they are. This is a difficult task if we are not to become apologists for the dominant culture expressed in our institutional affiliations or to become exponents of a new self-righteous ideology of globalization.

Walter Wink's work is especially helpful here in that he encourages us to understand the organic nature of our complicity with systems of dominance and simultaneously to realize how we can powerfully challenge these systems through our praxis. It is through our encounter with the other, particularly with the other who is the enemy, that we have the opportunity to engage that part of ourselves that we have disowned.[11] I argue that any time we deeply engage the other who has different presuppositions and cultural understandings than we do, we have the opportunity for both of us to become more fully human. Bridge-building is one way that we can institutionalize this encounter with the significant other. By systemically linking in respectful ways that honor the developmental contexts of all involved, persons and institutions who are significantly different from one another both can become more fully human.

We have just begun our journey developing a new way of being more fully human together. The shared praxis of those of us involved in this project goes far beyond my attempts to describe this experience. What we do have is a significant shared history of praxis both as individuals and as institutions, as well as the willingness to take the next steps together. The steps are not easy and the journey is long. Patricia Williams captures the difficulty of the task we have set for ourselves:

> It is this perspective, the ambivalent, multivalent way of seeing, that is at the core of what is called critical theory, feminist theory, and much of the minority critique of law. It has to do with a fluid positioning that sees back and forth across boundary, which acknowledges that I can be black and good and black and bad, and that I can also be black and white, male and female, yin and yang, love and hate.
>
> Nothing is simple. Each day is a new labor.[12]

Appendixes

Appendix A

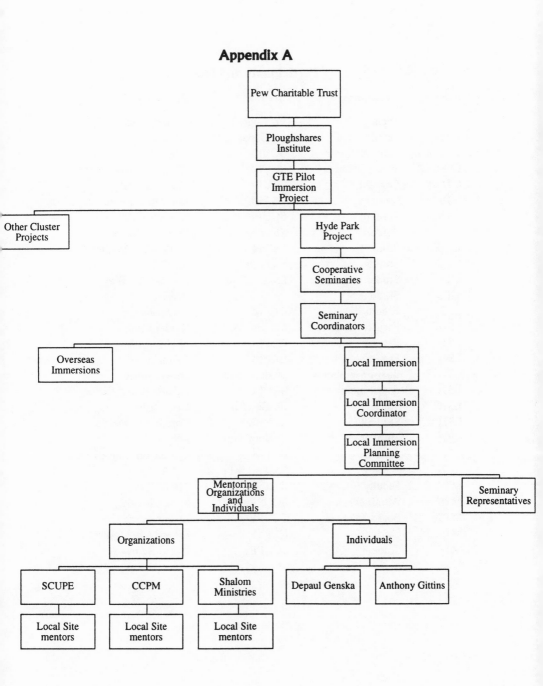

Appendix B
Participants and Sites

School	Relationship	Mentor	Placement Site
CTS	Faculty	Fr. Genska	Genesis Hse.
CTS	Faculty	Fr. Genska	Genesis Hse.
CTS	Administrator	SCUPE	AIDS PC Netw.
CTS	Board Member	SCUPE	"Bethel, Chgo. Hts."
CTS	Student	SCUPE	Project Equality
CTS	Student	CCPM	Interfaith Counc. Homeless
CTS	Student	SCUPE	Chicago Crist. Ind. League
CTS	Student	Shalom Min	Peoples Church
CTU	Student	CCPM	United Ch. Medical Ctr.
CTU	Student	Fr. Gittins	REST
CTU	Student	Shalom Min	Catholic Worker
CTU	Student	Fr. Gittins	REST
LSTC	Faculty	CCPM	Synapses
LSTC	Faculty	Shalom Min	Kovler Center
LSTC	Faculty	CCPM	Night Ministry
LSTC	Faculty	CCPM	CALC
LSTC	Board Member	Shalom Min	Unity House
LSTC	Board member	SCUPE	LaSalle (CYCLE)
LSTC	Student	Fr. Genska	Genesis Hse.
LSTC	Student	SCUPE	Cornell Baptist
LSTC	Student	Shalom Min	Am. Ind. Ctr
LSTC	Student	CCPM	United Ch. Rogers Park
MTS	Faculty	Shalom Min	TIAA
MTS	Faculty Spouse	Shalom Min	TIAA
MTS	Administrator	SCUPE	Rock Church
MTS	Board Member	SCUPE	Rock Church
MTS	Student	CCPM	United Ch. Medical Ctr.
MTS	Student	SCUPE	World Relief

Appendix C

GTE Initial Orientation–ICC
19–20 September, 1992

Saturday, 19 September
   9:00–10:00   Registration
   10:00–11:15
      Opening Prayer/Welcome—George Cairns
      ICC Guidelines
      Overview of Project—Susan Thistlethwaite
      Stories from Overseas Immersions
            Dow Edgerton
            Audrea Fumbanks
      Brief Overview of Local Immersion/Discuss Covenant forms
   11:15–12:15   Share why participating—in small groups
   12:15–1:00   Lunch
   1:00–1:30   What is Globalization?—Dr. Bob Schreiter
   1:30–1:50   Q & A
   1:50–2:00   Break
   2:00–3:30   Systems in the City—Dr. Stan Hallet
   3:30–3:40   Brief for Walk in Uptown
   3:40–4:00   Break
   4:00–6:00   A Walk in Uptown (Ecumenical Group facilitators meet)
   6:00–7:00   Supper
   7:00–9:00   Process in Small Groups
   9:00   R & R
Sunday, 20 September, 1992
   8:00–9:00   Breakfast
   9:00–12:00   Worship in the Neighborhood
      St. Thomas of Canterbury, 4827 N. Kenmore
            Hosts: Fr. Richard Simon and Ms. Wanda Joseph
            English Mass at 9:00
            Coffee Hour/Conversation: 10:00
      Peoples Church (UCC), 941 W. Lawrence Ave.
            Hosts: Rev. Marguerite Voelkel, Rev. Dr. George Cairns
            Tour of Church/Conversation: 9:30
            Worship: 11:00
      Uptown Ministries (Lutheran), 4720 N. Sheridan Road
            Host: Rev. Jerry Reimer
            Conversation: 9:30

163

Worship: 11:00
Buena Presbyterian, 4301 N. Sheridan Rd.
    Host: Rev. Langdon Hubbard
    Conversation: 9:30
    Worship: 10:45

12:30–1:00   Lunch
1:00–3:00   Listening to Voices from the Community
    Mr. Sam Keahna, Executive Director, American Indian Center
    Mr. Ron Kidd, Member of the Buddhist Council of the Midwest
    Dr. Ghulan Aasi, American Islamic College
    Rev. David Boyd, Executive Director, Unity House
    Rev. Nidza Lopez, Pastor, San Lucas UCC
3:00   Break
3:15–4:30   Small Group Processing
4:30–5:00   Participants meet with community coordinators (CCPM,
    SCUPE, etc.)
5:00–5:30   Initial covenant forms placed on altar as part of ceremony
5:30–6:00   Prepare to Depart
6:00–7:30   Supper at Pasteur Restaurant (next to People's Church)

Appendix D

"Celebrating Our Journey, Visioning the Future"

Globalization of Theological Education Celebration
A Joint Project of Catholic Theological Union, Chicago
Theological Seminary, Lutheran School of Theology at Chicago,
and McCormick Theological Seminary
Coordinated by The Pilot-Immersion Project
and Funded by the Pew Charitable Trust

Location: Catholic Theological Union
Time: 1:00–8:00 Friday, May 21, 1993

1:00–1:30   Welcomes/In gathering
Host: John M. Kaserow, Professor of Mission Studies and Coordinator of World
Mission Program, Catholic Theological Union
Native American Blessing: Sam Keahna, Director, American Indian Center
Donald Senior, President, Catholic Theological Union
Kathleen Hughes, Academic Dean, Catholic Theological Union

1:30–2:00   Globalization as a Concept and Practice
Keynote Speaker: Anthony Gittins, Professor of Theological Anthropology,
Catholic Theological Union

2:00–2:30   An Overview of the GTE Project
Overview of the National Project: David Roozen, Research Director, Pilot-Immersion
Project, Globalization in Theological Education
Overview of the Hyde Park Project: Yoshiro Ishida, Director, Center for Global
Mission; Lecturer in World Mission, Lutheran School of Theology at Chicago

2:30–3:30   Stories from the Overseas and Local Immersions
South-East Asia: Willliam R. Myers, Academic Dean, Chicago Theological Sem-
inary.
Africa: Jamie T. Phelps, Assistant Professor of Doctrinal Theology, Catholic
Theological Union
South America: Raleigh Hegwood, Trustee, McCormick Theological Seminary
Local Immersion in Chicago: Marilyn Olson, Student, Lutheran School of Theology
at Chicago

Introduction of: Daniel Gomez-Ibanez, Executive Director, Council for a Parlia-
ment of the World's Religions

3:30–3:50   Break

165

3:50–6:00   Informal Meetings
Meet with seminary planners regarding globalization planning, visit with community representatives and with international students

6:00–6:15   Break

6:15–7:00   Liturgy of
Repentance/Celebration/Commissioning/Covenanting

7:00–8:00   Celebratory Meal

Notes

1. Beyond Theological Tourism

1. Cynthia Enloe, *Bananas, Beaches and Bases: Making Feminist Sense of International Politics* (Berkeley, Ca.: University of California Press, 1990), 21.

2. Pico Iyer, *Video Night In Kathmandu and Other Reports from the No-So-Far East* (New York: Random House, 1989), 6–7.

3. Enloe, 20.

4. Enloe, 195.

5. Iyer, 6–7.

6. Martin Buber, *I and Thou* (New York: Scribners, 1988); *see also* Donald L. Beer, *Mutuality: The Vision of Martin Buber* (Albany, N.Y.: SUNY Press, 1985).

7. *See* Walter Farley, *Good and Evil: Interpreting a Human Condition* (Minneapolis, Minn.: Fortress, 1990), 39.

8. Susan Sontag, *AIDS and Its Metaphors* (New York: Farrar, Straus and Giroux, 1988), 40, 56.

9. Catherine Keller, *From Broken Web. Sexism, Separation and the Self* (Boston: Beacon Press, 1986), chap. 4, 155–215.

10. Ibid., 79.

11. Ada Maria Isasi-Diaz, "Solidarity: Love of Neighbor in the 1980's," In *Lift Every Voice: Constructing Christian Theologies from the Underside,* eds. Susan Brooks Thistlethwaite and Mary Potter Engel, (San Francisco: HarperSanFrancisco, 1990), 33.

3. Globalization in the Hyde Park Seminaries

1. Cited in Robert J. Schreiter, C.PP.S. "What is Globalization?" unpublished.

4. Education for Ministry

1. *See* Clinton E. Stockwell, "Urban Churches and Ministries (A Brief History)," and "Theodore Dwight Weld," in *Dictionary of Christianity in America,* edited by Daniel G. Reid (Downers Grove, Ill.: InterVarsity Press, 1990).

2. Clinton E. Stockwell, "A Better Class of People: Protestants in the Shaping of Early Chicago, 1833–1873," (unpublished Ph.D. dissertation: University of Illinois at Chicago, 1992).

3. For more information, see the book by two former seminary students and graduates of the Urban Training Center in Chicago, Alan B. Anderson and George W. Pickering, *Confronting the Color Line: The Broken Promise of the Civil Rights Movement in Chicago* (Athens, Ga.: University of Georgia Press, 1988).

4. This is captured in the work of another graduate of the former Urban Training Center in Chicago; John Hall Fish, *Black Power, White Control: The Struggle of The Woodlawn Organization of Chicago* (Princeton, N.J.: Princeton University Press, 1973); and Sanford D. Horwitt, *Let Them Call Me Rebel: Saul Alinsky—His Life and Legacy* (New York: Alfred A. Knopf, 1989).

5. For information on the Urban Training Center, see, George D. Younger, *From the New Creation to Urban Crisis: A History of Action Training Ministries, 1962–1975* (Chicago: Center for the Scientific Study of Religion, 1987).

6. For the spirit of this movement, consult Eldin Villafane, *The Liberating Spirit: Toward an Hispanic American Pentecostal Ethic* (New York: University Press of America, 1992).

7. For more information on the use of this methodology, see Younger, *From New Creation to Urban Crisis*, 22–28; and Harvey Cox, *The Secular City: Twenty-Fifth Anniversary Edition* (New York: Collier Books, 1990), 222–223.

8. This process, called the Pastoral or Hermeneutic circle, was made popular by Peter Henriot and Joe Holland, *Social Analysis: Linking Faith and Justice* (Maryknoll, N.Y.: Orbis Books, 1983). See also, David Kolb, *Experiential Learning: Experience as the Source of Learning and Development* (Englewood Cliffs, N.J.: Prentice-Hall, 1984). Kolb, an authority on experiential education, argues that there is a fourfold movement to the process of learning. These four components include 1) Concrete Experience, 2) Reflective Observation, 3) Abstract Conceptualization, and 4) Active Experimentation. Experiential learning generally acknowledges the importance of this process as identified by Kolb.

5. Transformation Education

1. Victor Turner, *The Ritual Process: Structure and Anti-Structure* (Ithaca, N.Y.: Cornell University Press, 1977).

2. Arnold van Gennep, *The Rites of Passage* (Chicago: University of Chicago Press, 1960).

3. Mircea Eliade, *Rites and Symbols of Initiation: The Mysteries of Birth and Rebirth* (New York: Harper Torchbooks, 1975).

4. Caroline Walker Bynum, "Women's Stories, Women's Symbols: A Critique of Victor Turner's Theory of Liminality," in *Anthropology and the Study of Religion,* ed. R. L. Moore and F. E. Reynolds (Chicago: Center for the Scientific Study of Religion, 1984), 105–119.

5. *See* Paulo Freire, *Pedagogy of the Oppressed* (New York: Seabury Press, 1970), and *Pedagogy of the City* (New York: Continuum Publishing Company, 1993).

6. Leonardo Boff, *Ecclesiogenesis: The Base Communities Reinvent the Church* (Maryknoll, N.Y.: Orbis Books, 1986), 23–33.

7. Ibid., 24–25.

8. *Association of Chicago Theological Schools Announcements,* ed. Jeannette F. Scholer (Chicago: n.p., 1992–93), 19.

9. Ibid., 20.

10. Claude-Marie Barbour, George Cairns, Nancy Cairns, and Eleanor Doidge, "Shalom Ministries: An Urban Base Community Comes of Age," *The Chicago Theological Seminary Register* 81, no. 1 (1991) 42–49.

11. GTE Grant proposal, March, 1988, p. 13.

12. W. F. Whyte and K. K. Whyte, *Making Mondragon: The Growth and Dynamics of the Worker Cooperative Complex* (Ithaca, N.Y.: New York School of Industrial and Labor Relations Press, 1988), 241.

6. Ministry on the Boundaries

1. Shalom Ministries, founded by Claude Marie in 1975, is an ecumenical covenant community in service to cultural groups and local communities. An important aspect of that service is training people for inner-city and cross-cultural ministries. Shalom Ministries was one of the field placements for the theological students, faculty, administrators, and trustees whose institutions participated in the GTE-LIP.

2. Robert A. Evans (1987) lists eight pedagogical components of the transformative process: encounter with the poor; experiential immersion that challenges assumptions; openness to vulnerability; community of support and accountability; vision and values; cycle of critical socioeconomic analysis; commitment, involvement, and leadership; and symbol, ritual, and liturgy. See Robert Evans, "Education for Emancipation," in *Pedagogies for the Non-Poor*, ed. Alice Evans, Robert Evans, and William B. Kennedy (Maryknoll, N.Y.: Orbis Books, 1987), 257–284.

In this chapter we will use the components delineated by Eleanor Doidge in "Personal Transformation toward Global Awareness: A Training Model for Cross-Cultural Mission and Ministry," unpublished D. Min. thesis (Chicago Theological Seminary, 1989), which bear some similarity to Evans' components.

3. We chose to use the term "the poor" more extensively than the terms "the oppressed" or "the marginalized," to focus more precisely on the gap in resources and life possibilities that exists between educators and students in theological schools and people in grassroots communities.

4. The metaphor of weaving has become popular in feminist writings in recent years. For a fuller explication of this metaphor and a demonstration of how it can be used to describe complex theological and relational processes, see Christine M. Smith. *Weaving the Sermon: Preaching in a Feminist Perspective.* Louisville, KY: Westminster/John Knox Press, 1989. For Claude Marie, the metaphor evokes memories of life in Africa, for Eleanor, memories of life in South America, and for Peggy, memories of life in the Fort Berthold Indian Reservation, North Dakota. In each setting, the weaving of indigenous women was an important dimension of communal experience.

5. Mark Kline Taylor, *Remembering Esperanza: A Cultural-Political Theology North American Praxis* (Maryknoll, N.Y.: Orbis Books, 1990), 23.

6. Taken from the final conversation with Barbara about her project to develop

a Board of Directors and African-American leadership for the St. Elizabeth Catholic Worker House, April 24, 1993.

7. Ibid.

8. This quote and the following ones in this vignette were taken from excerpts of the closing meeting of the LIP volunteers who had been placed in Shalom Ministries, May 14, 1993.

9. Walter Brueggemann, *Biblical Reflections on Shalom: Living Towards a Vision* (Philadelphia: United Church Press, 1976).

10. Claude Marie Barbour, George Cairns, Nancy Cairns, and Eleanor Doidge, "Shalom Ministries: An Urban Base Community Comes of Age," *The Chicago Theological Seminary Register* 81, no. 1 (1991): 42–49.

11. Jerry Folk, "Salvation as Shalom," *Dialog* 26, no. 2 (1987): 108.

12. The term "dialogue" is used here in the manner discussed by David J. Bosch in his address, "The Church in Dialogue: From Self Delusion to Vulnerability," given to the World Mission Institute, April 9–11, 1987, in Chicago, Illinois.

13. Earlier versions of the Shalom principles can be found in the Shalom By-laws, Article II, Section I, 1980.

14. Taken from Shalom community discussions, 1987.

15. Barbour, 305

16. Ibid. "Such a model of ministry is based solidly on the model of Christ himself who 'became poor for [our] sake, to make [us] rich out of his poverty' (II Cor. 8:9). The whole thrust of the incarnation is that God takes us seriously enough to enter our world; God cares enough for us to become one of us, to stand at our side."

17. Gustavo Gutierrez, *The Power of the Poor in History* (London: SCM, 1983), 211.

18. From an interview with George Cairns, Terry Bozich, and seven residents at the Northmere Hotel, Uptown, Chicago, IL., May 24, 1993.

19. Paulo Freire, *Pedagogy of the Oppressed* (New York: Seabury Press, 1968)

20. National Federation of Priests' Council, *Developing Basic Christian Communities—A Handbook* (1979); *Pro Mundi Vita Bulletin* 62 (September, 1976).

21. James E. Hug, ed., *Tracing the Spirit* (New York: Paulist Press, 1983), 7.

22. Robert Schreiter, *Constructing Local Theologies* (Maryknoll, N.Y.: Orbis Books, 1985), 29.

23. Claude Marie Barbour, "Seeking Justice and Shalom in the City," *International Review of Mission* 73 (July, 1984): 303–309; Schreiter, *Constructing Local Theologies*.

24. Morton uses the term "hearing into speech" to refer to the process of listening with one's whole heart and attention to another as a crucial step in human empowerment.

25. Barbour, (1984): 308.

26. Evaluation session with Sam Keahna, Mark Thompson, Claude Marie Barbour, and Eleanor Doidge.

27. Archie Smith, Jr., *The Relational Self: Ethics and Therapy from a Black Church Perspective* (Nashville, Tenn.: Abingdon, 1982), 14.

28. Donald Batchelder, "Preparation for Cross-Cultural Experience," in *Beyond Experience: The Experiential Approach to Cross-Cultural Education,* ed. Donald Batchelder and Elizabeth W. Warner (Brattleboro, Ver.: The Experiment Press, 1977), 59–68.

29. Edward Hall, *Beyond Culture* (New York: Anchor Books, 1977), 281–283.

30. Claude-Marie Barbour, "Jesus, Shalom, and Rites of Passage: A Journey Toward Global Mission and Spirituality," *Missiology: An International Review,* 15, no. 3 (July, 1987): 311.

31. Ibid, 311.

7. Persons in Female Prostitution

1. Over the years I discovered others who had interpreted this world for readers. Among the helpful works were Jennifer James, *The Politics of Prostitution* (Seattle: 1977), and Vern Bullough, *History of Prostitution* (New Hyde Park, N.Y.: University Books, 1964).

2. Genesis House, 911 West Addison Avenue, Chicago, IL 60613. Numerous documents and printed materials both on Genesis House itself and its ministry, and on prostitution, are available by writing to Genesis House.

3. Edwina Gateley. *I Hear a Seed Growing* (Trabuco, Calif.: Source Books, 1990).

4. "Prostitutes Anonymous" is a twelve-step program for women trying to leave the life of prostitution and engage in more life-giving lifestyles. Further information may be obtained from Prostitutes Anonymous, 11225 Magnolia Blvd., North Hollywood, CA 91601.

5. Jean Guy Nadeu, "Pastoral Inculturation with Regard to Prostitution," (Paper delivered at Catholic Theological Society Convention, San Francisco, June 1990).

6. Paul Kinsie and Charles Winick, *The Lively Commerce* (Chicago: Quadrangle Books, 1971).

7. "Johns Anonymous" is a fellowship of men who have frequented the services of prostitutes and who, realizing their addiction, have formed this twelve-step supportive fellowship. Further information may be obtained from: Rev. Alquin Coyle, O.F.M., St. Francis Church, 135 West 31st Street, New York, NY 10001. Anonymity is a principle. Fr. Coyle will forward your request to Johns Anonymous, which meets regularly at St. Francis Church in New York City.

8. "Sex for Sale: An Alarming Boom in Prostitution Debases the Women and Children of the World," *Time,* 21 June 1993.

9. For lists of names and addresses of individuals or agencies who work with persons in female prostitution, please contact Fr. Depaul Genska, O.F.M., Catholic Theological Union, 5401 S. Cornell, Chicago, IL 60615. Phone: (312) 753–5315.

10. Doris Donnelly, "Pilgrims and Tourists: Conflicting Metaphors for the Christian Journey to God," *Spirituality Today* 44, 1 (Spring 1992).

8. A Matter of Homelessness

1. Danny L. Jorgensen, *Participant Observation: A Methodology for Human Studies* (Newbury Park, Calif.: Sage Publications, 1989), 8.

2. Ioan Lewis, *Social Anthropology in Perspective* (Harmondsworth, England: Penguin, 1976) 24.

3. John Beattie, *Other Cultures* (New York: Free Press, 1964), 87.

4. Beattie, 37–38.

5. *International Encyclopedia of the Social Sciences* 11: 240 (New York: Macmillan), s.v. "participant observation."

6. Jorgensen, 13.

7. Jorgensen, 38.

8. Michael Jackson, *Paths Toward a Clearing: Radical Empiricism and Ethnographic Inquiry* (Bloomington: Indiana Univ. Press, 1989).

9. Caroline Bynum, "Women's Stories, Women's Symbols: A Critique of Victor Turner's Theory of Liminality," in *Fragmentation and Redemption* (New York: Zone Books, 1992), 27–51.

10. Peter Berger and T. Luckmann. *The Social Construction of Reality* (Harmondsworth, England: Penguin, 1971).

10. Mentoring for Transformation

1. I would particularly like to thank Rev. Marguerite Voelkel, pastor of preaching and administration at Peoples Church of Chicago, for her continuous support of this ministry. I would also like to thank my other colleagues in ministry and the congregation at Peoples Church for their help and assistance.

2. Kelson, A. H., Spiselman, A., Novick, D., and Klimovich, D., *Chicago Magazine's Guide to Chicago* (Chicago: Contemporary Books, 1983), 238.

3. Two grants from the Presbytery of Chicago "Self Development of People" program assisted in this work.

4. I am convinced that poorly coordinated and sometimes genuinely inadequate health care led to unnecessary deaths among my friends.

5. I am indebted to my friend Dr. Bonganjalo Goba, a member of Shalom Ministries, who has described these experiences in his South African context.

6. I find an extremely helpful analysis of structural evil along with suggestions for ways of engaging it in Walter Wink's *Jesus' Third Way: Violence and Nonviolence in South Africa* (Santa Cruz, Calif.: New Society Publishers, 1987).

7. In his more recent work, Wink further details his analysis of evil and examines ways in which structural evil has impact on those engaged in action resisting it. Walter Wink, *Engaging the Powers: Discernment and Resistance in a World of Domination* (Minneapolis, Minn.: Fortress Press, 1992).

8. Mohandas K. Gandhi, *An Autobiography: The Story of My Experiments With Truth* (Boston, Mass.: Beacon Press, 1957).

9. Morris Berman, in his work: *The Reenchantment of the World* (Ithaca, N.Y.: Cornell University Press, 1981); and *Coming to Our Senses: Body and Spirit in the Hidden History of the West* (New York: Simon & Schuster, 1989), offers us a new epistemology of relationship and full-bodied engagement.

10. Aaron Milavec, *To Empower as Jesus Did: Acquiring Spiritual Power Through Apprenticeship*. Toronto Studies in Theology, Volume 9 (New York: The Edwin Mellen Press, 1982).

11. Milavec, 3.

12. Milavec, 191.

13. Here too, I am indebted to the work of Morris Berman which encouraged me to closely examine Gregory Bateson's ideas regarding education and learning.

14. Gregory Bateson, *Steps to an Ecology of Mind*. (Northvale, N.J.: Jason Aronson, 1987) 279.

15. Bateson, 280.

16. Here language poses difficulties. "Higher" and "lower" carry much surplus meaning with them, with "higher" suggesting "better" or more "spiritual" values and "lower" suggesting "poorer" or more "profane" ones. Not understanding that all levels of learning are always available to us has caused countless suffering and misplaced effort. Just as the class "furniture" is no better or worse than the subclass included within it, "chair", so too Learning III and IV are no better or worse than Learning I or II. All are part of the human experience and equally important. It is precisely the *awareness that this is the case* that is difficult for us to profoundly experience and understand.

17. Bateson, 287.

18. Bateson, 292–293.

19. Bateson, 300.

20. Bateson, 300.

21. Bateson, 301.

22. Bateson, 297.

23. Bateson, 293.

24. Bateson, *Steps*, 301.

25. Bateson, *Steps*, 293. Here Bateson states that "Learning IV would be a change in Learning III, but probably does not occur in any adult living organism on this earth." He proposes that "Evolutionary process has, however, created organisms whose ontogeny brings them to Level III. The combination of phylogenesis with ontogenesis, in fact, achieves Level IV." Here I am using the term, Learning IV, to describe a process that *does* occur occasionally in adult human beings.

26. For another view of Jesus as transformative educator, see Walter Wink's *Jesus' Third Way*.

27. Thomas Del Prete, *Thomas Merton and the Education of the Whole Person* (Birmingham, Ala.: Religious Education Press, 1990) 100.

28. Milavec, 173.

11. Individual and Social Transformation

1. Walter Wink, *Engaging the Powers: Discernment and Resistance in a World of Domination*. (Minneapolis, Minn.: Fortress Press, 1992).

2. Here are Bateson's criteria for mind from *Mind and Nature: A Necessary Unity* (New York: E. P. Dutton, 1979), 92. "1) A mind is an aggregate of interacting parts or components. 2) The interaction between parts of mind is triggered by difference, and difference is a non-substantial phenomenon not located in space or time; difference is related to negentropy and entropy rather than to energy. 3) Mental process requires collateral energy. 4) Mental process requires circular (or more complex) chains of determination. 5) In mental process, the effects of difference are to be regarded as transforms (i.e., coded versions) of events which preceded them. The rules of such transformation must be comparatively stable (i.e., more stable than the content) but are themselves subject to transformation. 6)

The description and classification of these processes of transformation disclose a hierarchy of logical types immanent in the phenomena."

3. Gregory Bateson and Mary Catherine Bateson, *Angels Fear: Towards an Epistemology of the Sacred* (New York: Macmillan Publishing Company, 1987) 19. " . . . there is no requirement of a clear boundary, like a surrounding envelope of skin or membrane, and you can recognize that this definition (of mind) includes only some of the characteristics of what we call 'life'. As a result it applies to a much wider range of those complex phenomena called 'systems', including systems consisting of multiple organisms or systems in which some of the parts are living and some are not, or even to systems in which there are no living parts."

4. William Ernest Hocking, "Some Second Principles," in eds. George P. Adams and William Pepperel Montague, *Contemporary American Philosophy*, 1, (New York: Russell & Russell, 1962, first published 1930), 391–392, cited by Margaret Lewis Furse in "Experience and Certainty: William Ernest Hocking and Philosophical Mysticism," *AAR Studies in Religion*, 50 (Atlanta, Ga.: Scholars Press, 1988), 49.

5. Leonardo Boff, *Ecclesiogenesis: The Base Communities Reinvent the Church* (Maryknoll, N.Y.: Orbis Books, 1986).

6. *The Compact Edition of the Oxford English Dictionary*, Vol. II (New York: Oxford University Press, 1981), 2723.

7. Gregory Bateson, *Steps to an Ecology of Mind: Collected Essays in Anthropology, Psychiatry, Evolution, and Epistemology* (Northvale, N.J.: Jason Aronson, 1987), 155.

8. A number of studies describe these maps. I am just beginning to reflect on how the following sources may help further inform our praxis. *See* Marcia Baxter Magolda, *Knowing and Reasoning in College: Gender-Related Patterns in Students' Intellectual Development* (San Francisco: Jossey-Bass, 1992); M. F. Belenky, B. M. Clinchy, N. Goldberger, and J. M. Tarule, *Women's Ways of Knowing: The Development of Self, Voice, and Mind* (New York: Basic Books, 1986); Carol Gilligan, *In a Different Voice: Psychological Theory and Women's Development.* (Cambridge, Mass.: Harvard University Press, 1982); Joel Kegan, *The Evolving Self: Problem and Process in Human Development* (Cambridge, Mass.: Harvard University Press, 1982); D. J. Levinson, *The Seasons of a Man's Life* (New York: Ballantine Books, 1979); William G. Perry, *Forms of Intellectual and Ethical Development in the College Years: A Scheme* (New York: Harcourt Brace Jovanovich College Publishers, 1968).

9. Laurent A. Daloz, *Effective Teaching and Mentoring: Realizing the Transformative Power of Adult Learning Experiences* (San Francisco: Jossey-Bass, 1986).

10. Daloz, 81.

11. Wink, 263–77.

12. Patricia D. Williams, *The Alchemy of Race and Rights* (Cambridge: Harvard University Press, 1991), 130.